THE BEST
GRAND STAIRCASE-ESCALANTE NATIONAL MONUMENT HIKES

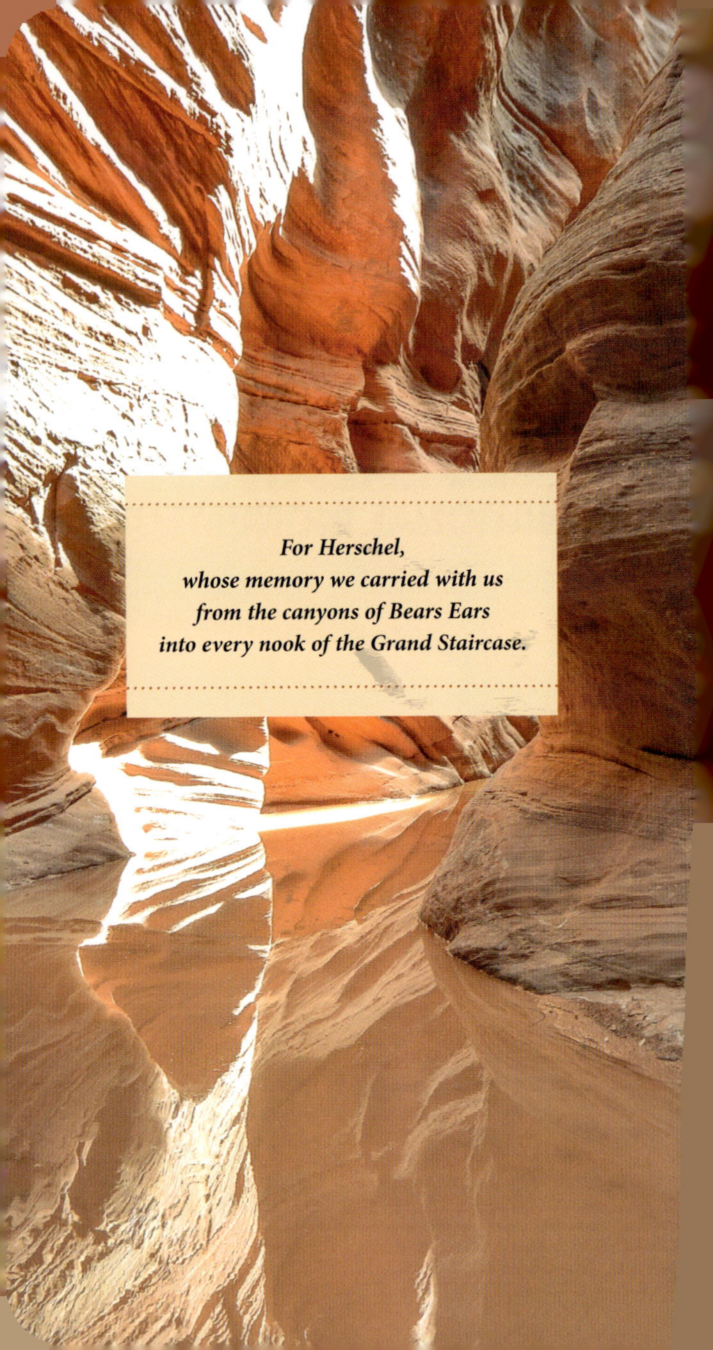

For Herschel,
whose memory we carried with us
from the canyons of Bears Ears
into every nook of the Grand Staircase.

COLORADO
MOUNTAIN CLUB
PACK GUIDE

THE BEST GRAND STAIRCASE-ESCALANTE NATIONAL MONUMENT HIKES

MORGAN SJOGREN and MICHAEL VERSTEEG

The Colorado Mountain Club Press
Golden, Colorado

The Best Grand Staircase-Escalante National Monument Hikes
© 2019 by Morgan Sjogren and Michael VerSteeg

PUBLISHED BY

The Colorado Mountain Club Press
710 Tenth Street, Suite 200, Golden, Colorado 80401
303-996-2743   email: cmcpress@cmc.org
website: http://www.cmc.org

CORRECTIONS: We greatly appreciate when readers alert us to errors
or outdated information by contacting us at cmcpress@cmc.org.

Morgan Sjogren and Michael VerSteeg: photographers
Takeshi Takahashi: designer
Mira Perrizo: copyeditor
Jeff Golden: publisher

"I have seen almost more beauty than I can bear."
—Everett Ruess

COVER PHOTO: Morgan Sjogren

DISTRIBUTED TO THE BOOK TRADE BY
Mountaineers Books, 1001 Klickitat Way, Suite 201, Seattle, WA
98134, 800-553-4453, www.mountaineersbooks.org

We gratefully acknowledge the financial support of the people of Colorado through the Scientific and Cultural Facilities District of greater metropolitan Denver for our publishing activities.

TOPOGRAPHIC MAPS are created with CalTopo.com software.

WARNING: Hiking, canyoneering, backpacking, swimming, rafting, and other outdoor pursuits are high-risk activities. This guidebook is not a substitute for experience, training and common sense. The users of this guidebook assume full responsibility for their own safety. Weather, terrain conditions, and individual experience and abilities must be considered before undertaking any of the outings in this guide. The Colorado Mountain Club and the author do not assume any liability for injury, death, damage to property, or violation of the law that may result from the use of this book.

Printed in Korea

ISBN: 978-0-9842213-7-0

Revised edition 2022

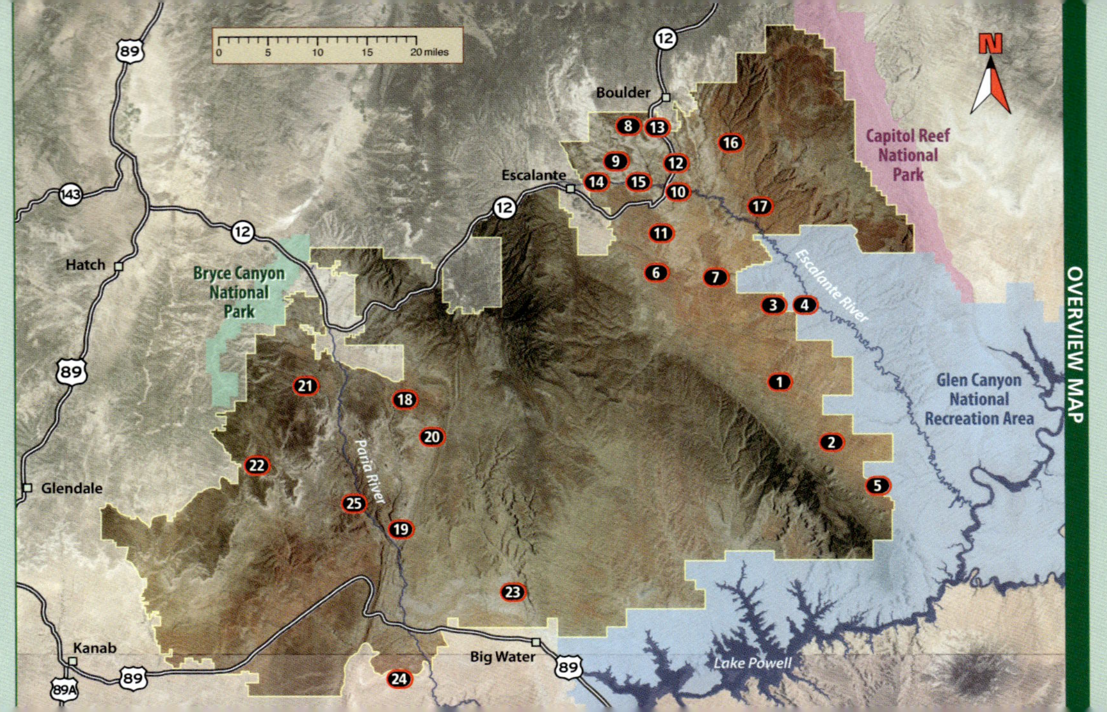
N
20 miles
15
10
5
0
Boulder
Capitol Reef National Park
Escalante
Hatch
Bryce Canyon National Park
Glendale
Escalante River
Glen Canyon National Recreation Area
Paria River
Kanab
Big Water
Lake Powell
89
143
12
89
12
12
16
8
13
9
12
14
15
10
17
11
6
7
3
4
1
2
5
21
18
20
22
25
19
23
24
89
89A
89

CONTENTS

THE HIKES

Foreword

Disclaimer: There are no secrets in this guidebook. There aren't many secrets anymore anyway, thanks to the Internet. After all, if you are looking for "the one" secret spot in a guidebook, you're sniffing down the wrong route to begin with. There are mysteries and magic to be found in every nook, twist, and cell of this place. Slow down, smell the plants, drink from a seep beneath a hanging garden, slither across the slickrock with the collared lizards, listen to the chorus of toads, hug a hot sunbaked rock. In time, the desert will share its secrets.

Writing a guidebook may appear as an odd response to President Trump's reduction of Grand Staircase-Escalante National Monument (as well as Bears Ears National Monument) in 2017. However, as the monument's protection sat in limbo, the media spotlight drove unprecedented interest and visitation to Grand Staircase-Escalante, and with it the great need for accurate, educational, conservation-minded material to help people respectfully visit this incredible and endangered place, while informing about current events and the complex system of public lands of which Grand Staircase-Escalante is a part.

As such, our mission was not merely to guide hikers through sensuously sculpted sandstone slots, verdant canyons, and windswept mesas that take the breath away. This book is not a stack of directions, it's a hiking companion.

The hidden charms of Grand Staircase—the slot canyons, swimming holes, geological formations, paleontological discoveries, numerous endangered species, Indigenous homelands, and human history—are enough to keep everyone, from the casual tourists to the filthy desert rats, coming back for more. For most, a trip here will involve hiking a few short slot canyons in between long stretches driving across the Devil's Backbone or along The Cockscomb. Lackadaisical roadside entertainment abounds from imagination-inducing rock formations to ancient handprints strewn across sandstone walls.

ACKNOWLEDGMENTS

A huge thank you to the Grand Staircase-Escalante Partners, Glen Canyon Conservancy, Martin Stamat, R.E. Burrillo, Katja Knoll, David Roberts, and all who helped contribute research materials, support, and advice, along with fighting the good fight to protect GSENM and public lands. To everyone who let us crash in your spare room, let us shower, gave us tips, gave us critiques, fed us, and shared miles with us, it is greatly appreciated.

Morgan—

To my family—Mom, Dad, Uncle Bill, Aunty Kristy, and my dear friends scattered across the country—thank you for keeping this wild Jeepsy rooted even when I roamed far from you all during this project. I felt your love and support in every step. The Colorado Mountain Club first proposed the outlandish idea to write a guidebook for Bears Ears National Monument during its most tumultuous hour. That project beautifully changed the course and location of my life. I am grateful for your faith and willingness to go forward with my idea for this guide immediately after Grand Staircase-Escalante NM's unprecedented reduction. David and Sharon Roberts, meeting you in Bears Ears during the editing phase was a delightful surprise. Your insight helped my nerves from rolling off a cliff as I wrestled with the dusty demons that accompanied working through this book. David's contribution to these pages is a gift I am so grateful for. Ralph—comrade and friend in defense of sacred wilderness, thank you for sharing your words in these pages and surviving "Camp Snowball" with me during the biggest winter in Cedar Mesa history as I completed this guidebook. Mike, in Bears Ears you were an unexpected companion, and by the time we migrated to Grand Staircase you were a full-fledged co-author in a place we are both captivated by, yet are just barely beginning to know. Amongst the muck, mire, scrapes, and cow patties, that the scorching earth of canyon country threw at us, we certainly made our way through.

Lastly, to Grand Staircase-Escalante, Bears Ears, and the Colorado Plateau—you have stolen my heart and opened up a place for me to call home—for that I humbly and gratefully give you my words.

Michael—

Mom, everything I have done is inspired by your grit, including this project. Dad, for reminding me to not take things too seriously, lighten up, and things are always better beer in hand. Dave and Jean Mcgee, your support over the years is immeasurable. Tom Alward, James Madson, and Nicolau Beneria Myer for joining us in the canyons. Paco Cantu for inspiring me to take writing seriously. Lastly, of course, Morgan Sjogren, for sharing this project with me. We've spent eons in these canyons, scratching, clawing, and swimming through endless pools of muck, and somehow came out clean on the other side.

Guidebooks:
A Way to Wilderness

It's fair to say that neither Morgan nor I are inherently pro guidebooks. We have certainly wrestled with the idea of encouraging more visitors to a sensitive area that we love and care about. It wasn't until our work last year on the Bears Ears book, and the endless wormhole of understanding our public lands and the agencies that govern them, that I came to realize what a guidebook could be. Forever associated with giving away local "secrets," guidebooks and their authors are often shunned and unfairly blamed for the higher traffic, looting, ecological impacts, and loss of wilderness that comes with it.

I have come to believe that guidebooks are an effect of increased recreation in an area, not the other way around, and can provide a unique platform for the authors that write them to be voices for stewardship, responsible low-impact recreation, and wilderness. These books find their ways into the hands of thousands of visitors every year, and as such, create a rare opportunity to educate the public on how to protect an area, not just from developers and resource extraction, but also from ourselves.

It is a general public misconception that federal institutions such as the Forest Service and the Bureau of Land Management exist to preserve and protect an area. These institutions largely still operate on the principles of the era in which they were founded, and the word "conservation" in Teddy Roosevelt's day simply meant a conservation of *resources*, not the preservation of wilderness. While wilderness and preservation are important pillars of both the Forest Service and the BLM, they, along with recreation, constitute a new ethos considering public lands, and can often be conflictual with more historical methods of 'multi-use.'

In 1964, congress passed **The Wilderness Act**, defining wilderness as,

> A wilderness, in contrast with those areas where man and his own works dominate the landscape, is hereby recognized as an area where the earth and its community of life are untrammeled by man, where man himself is a visitor who does not remain.

Written by Howard Zahniser and heavily influenced by such figures of the day as Wally Stegner, The Wilderness Act recognized even in the 1950s the need for land jurisdictions that protected areas, not just from grazing and mineral and resource extraction, but also from the often uncontrolled and disruptive behavior of "high-impact" recreation, which has run rampant in our National Parks, National Monuments, and National Recreation Areas.

Today, The Wilderness Act of 1964 protects over **100 million acres** of federal land, and is without a doubt the most significant legislation passed by Congress preserving our national landscapes and heritage. But that path to declaring new wilderness areas is difficult. Not only do considered landscapes need to meet a number of qualifying conditions to even be considered wilderness, they also have to be approved by Congress, which in today's world is a difficult proposition.

As stated earlier, the Forest Service and BLM operate on a "multi-use" ethos that has largely governed their policies and shaped the economies and traditions of the western United States. Grazing, hardrock mining, logging, oil and gas extraction, and any other exploitative uses have historically dominated the policies and management of our public lands. Recreation, although by far the most economically lucrative, least subsidized, and least invasive of these activities, is without a doubt the new kid on the block, and hasn't been fully integrated into the BLM's antiquated use plans.

It is here that low-impact recreation has a unique opportunity, in the eyes of the BLM, to enhance value of the landscape as wilderness, rather than the resources that can be extracted from beneath it. In order to be considered for wilderness designation, the proposed lands must meet the following conditions:

> Minimal human imprint
> Opportunities for unconfined recreation
> At least five thousand acres
> Educational, scientific, or historical value

The idea that public land can be set aside **without use or management** is not an idea the BLM or any other governing agency dares to consider, therefore lands that we wish to designate as wilderness must appear to have value laid out by the criteria above. It is here that low-impact recreation is not just an opportunity, but also a **necessity** in preserving these landscapes.

It is here where I began to think of guidebooks in a new way. It is here where I began to feel differently about keeping my favorite spots "secret." It is here that I realized that the more people care about an area, the more likely it is to be set aside and protected. That the more people who visit with respect, and practice low-impact tactics and Leave No Trace ethics, the more value the BLM will see in designating Wilderness Study Areas, and maybe one day full-on Wilderness designation.

That in order to stop the BLM from putting in "high-impact recreation" infrastructure, maybe there are more people that are willing to hike in with a pack than there are that want to drive in with their RVs. And the more people that do so, and respect and get to know these places with their own two eyes and their own two legs, then the more people there will be to stand up for a designation, protect a place, and encourage public officials to push for Wilderness designations, before the developers and extractors get to it.

I ask you to consider that maybe that secret spot of yours, which likely is not a secret, could have a better chance of survival if more people cared about it. In the 1960s, the Grand Canyon was a National Park, but not free from developers and resource "conservationists." Proposed hydroelectric and water storage projects such as the Marble Canyon Dam and Bridge Canyon Dam would have flooded Marble Canyon (the upper portion of the Grand Canyon), diverted the Colorado River to the stagnant lake flooding the lower Grand Canyon by the Bridge Canyon Dam, and would have forever changed our national wonder into a series of stagnant irrigation reservoirs. However, these projects were met with obvious backlash and outcries from not just preservation activists but from the public as a whole. The Grand Canyon was and is part of our national identity, and people could not imagine flooding that

Steer clear of the crustbusters.

treasure. These projects were eventually abandoned after public outcry and support were enough to topple the developers.

Unfortunately, the public backlash against the development of the Grand Canyon came from a hard lesson learned years earlier. Just upstream of the Grand Canyon lied the less popular, and seldom seen Glen Canyon. Today there are few still living that ever saw, explored, or floated down the now flooded canyon. When Glen Canyon Dam was proposed in the 1950's, it was paired with a series of dams that would have flooded modern day Echo Canyon in Dinosaur National Monument. It is here the environmental groups such as The Sierra Club made that now oh-so-regrettable compromise that would forever alter the southwest and its great muddy river. The deal allowed the building of Glen Canyon Dam, in effect sacrificing Glen Canyon in order to save Echo Canyon, and its National Monument. It was an audacious move. The project was permitted even without the general support of the public or the small collective of people who knew Glen Canyon best (including the major leaders and activists in the Sierra Club at the time). Had Glen Canyon had the notoriety of its sister canyon upstream, or dare I say its National Monument status, one could perhaps still visit those deep dark canyons that are now lost beneath a sea of powerboats and irrigation runoff.

Glen Canyon Dam and Lake Powell, which it created, are concrete examples of what can happen to a place that is not considered valuable to low-impact recreation and wilderness preservation.The worst *can* happen, and it likely would have been much worse downriver if the public did not have the knowledge and appreciation that they did for the Grand Canyon.

With these ideas hanging overhead, Morgan and I both went back and forth over whether to include, exclude, or simply mention each hike in this book. Do we continue to send people to the most popular hikes and hopefully the low-impact ethos stays intact, or do we encourage exploration of the threatened areas, hoping recreation can get a better stronghold in the area. It's an ongoing discussion.

I'd wager those that knew Glen Canyon would have happily given up their "secret spot" if it meant they could still go there. We have an astounding gift as citizens of this country in our public lands, and one that should not be taken for granted. I for one believe that all lands that still meet the criteria of Wilderness should be designated as such, for once it is gone there is no going back. These are not designations that can be made retroactively and I only hope that we—the desert rats, the mountaineers, and the river dogs—take this responsibility seriously and do what we can today, before the developers flood our canyons and topple our mountains.

If we can, however, get more people to care about this landscape, we hope this book will be used as a tool in how to visit responsibly, and equip the reader with the knowledge on how to protect this area. Then, maybe, it makes a small difference. A small step to preventing another Glen Canyon Dam, to preventing another uranium or coal mine, or to halt construction of a tramway to the bottom of the Grand Canyon.

We frequently get asked, "What can I do to help?," especially with the current political fiasco surrounding Bears Ears and Grand Staircase. The answer is easy. Go there. Float these rivers, climb these cliffs, and scrape through these slots. Get in a fight with a park ranger and chase the cows. And don't ever forget that these are your **PUBLIC** lands.

Using This Guidebook

This guidebook offers a selection of Grand Staircase-Escalante's supposed 25 best non-technical hikes, which is an arbitrary and nearly impossible distinction to make. During the creation of this book we hiked countless routes and variations, yet still felt as though we were barely scratching the surface. It is our hope that this book serves as a starter manual for those wishing to get their feet wet in the area (and hopefully in the Escalante River and the pools in a slot canyon or two). The selection of routes ranges from short family-friendly day hikes to overnight and multi-day backpacking trips, and some terrain that is as demanding as possible to cover on foot without the use of ropes and other aids. That said, if you enjoy multi-sport experiences (especially canyoneering, packrafting, climbing, and mountain biking), these routes are likely to get your wheels turning with ways you can link routes together and move through the terrain with fewer limitations.

Read the route descriptions carefully and make your decisions based on the type of experience you wish to have. Be honest about you and your group's abilities. Fitness is not a replacement for experience and skill. Check the current weather and trail conditions before setting out. Every single route offers something special, and no one stands above the rest. You certainly will not gain much (at least much good) from a route that does not serve your abilities or the current conditions. Be forewarned that only one trip to the region is likely to leave you unsatisfied and craving more. Grand Staircase-Escalante would be impossible to explore and experience in its entirety in several lifetimes. It is our hope that your visit is memorable in such a way that it encourages you to think deeper, and perhaps even act, with regard to the role that public lands and wilderness play in our lives, and our impact on these precious spaces.

Hiking Essentials

There is freedom in the simple pursuit of setting out into the wilderness with little more than some rubber soles on your feet and a rucksack on your back. This is not an exhaustive gear checklist, but a list of basic recommended gear and considerations for hiking within GSENM.

1. **Navigation**—In addition to this guidebook, *always* bring a topo map and compass. Do familiarize yourself with how to use them ahead of time. GPS and other modern navigation tools may not work without cell reception or in tight canyons, nor will their charge last for the duration of many routes. Lastly, do as much research as possible about your route before your trip.

2. **Water and Filtration System**—While natural water sources exist in many places in GSENM, this is still the desert where dehydration is a common cause of death. Always bring your own supply of water for before, during, and after your hikes. A water filtration and treatment system is a must if you plan to drink from any creeks, streams, springs, seeps, or rivers.

3. **First Aid Supplies**—In case of an emergency you will be your first line of treatment in the backcountry. A basic first aid kit should include: antiseptic wipes, antibacterial ointment (e.g. bacitracin), adhesive bandages, butterfly bandages/adhesive wound-closure strips, gauze pads, non-

Slippin' and smilin' into Death Hollow.

stick sterile pads, medical adhesive tape, blister treatment, Ibuprofen/other pain-relief medication, insect sting relief treatment, antihistamine to treat allergic reactions, small knife, splinter (fine-point) tweezers, and safety pins.

4. **Sun Protection**—Sunscreen, sunglasses, and loose layers of clothing will protect you from sunburn and heat-related illnesses.

5. **Insulation**—Always bring a light jacket (at very least) and extra dry layers for hikes involving water. This is important even during the warmest months of the year as temperatures can drop drastically at night. Wetsuits are often needed in water-filled slot canyons, especially those that require swimming. One of the most common causes of death in the desert is hypothermia!

6. **Extra Fuel**—A good stash of snacks with high caloric densities are just as important for safety as for morale. While you can certainly splurge on fancy sports nutrition products, our favorite adventure fuel includes candy bars, toaster pastries, sardines, beer, fruit snacks, and home-made burritos. Also, be sure to lace your water with a powdered sports drink both to optimize hydration

Fuel your engine.

and for added energy via carbohydrates. Don't forget fuel for your vehicle, too—gas stations are often long distances from the trailheads. It's a good idea to top off whenever you get a chance and even carry a spare five-gallon container.

7. **Proper Footwear**—The hikes in Grand Staircase-Escalante are mostly technical and on rough terrain and often involve water. Look for a quality pair of hiking boots, hiking sandals,

or trail running shoes with an aggressive tread. Size your shoes carefully, and consider sock weight and foot swelling, to prevent black toenails and other nasty foot maladies. It is also recommended that you break your shoes in before your hikes to ensure that they fit properly and do not irritate your feet. As a rule, the shoe that you perceive to be most comfortable (and that is designed for the given activity) will be the best shoe.

Choose comfy cruisers.

8. **Headlamp/Batteries/Fire Starter**—Sometimes (usually) hikes take longer than planned. Having a headlamp (and extra batteries) helps ensure that you can navigate terrain safely in the dark. Having a fire starting option (lighter or matches) could also save your life if you do find yourself stranded overnight. Be sure to always check fire regulations and practice fire safety.

9. **Permits**—This requirement varies with each route. Permits are necessary for most overnight backcountry travel and are usually obtainable at the trailhead. See "Permits and Ranger Stations" for more details.

10. **Appetite For Adventure**—Many of the routes in this book will challenge you in a variety of ways, and even the easiest of hikes can prove difficult in some conditions. Aside from beautiful scenery and iconic destinations, the adventure itself is a part of the experience. An open mind and a smile will go a long way—especially when the weather is hot, the snacks are melted, and the water runs dry. Preparing yourself with these essentials will improve the quality and safety of your hike; however, a positive attitude will not only help you complete the route (if it's in the cards at all) but will also help retain the best types of memories long after you leave.

Love This Land: Leave No Trace

When President Clinton set aside the original 1.8 million acres of land for Grand Staircase-Escalante National Monument, he did not do so to create an outdoor playground, but rather to protect a sensitive area of land immensely valuable for scientific and archaeological research. Be sure to lessen the impact of your visit on the areas that you explore by following Leave No Trace principles along with other measures of respect listed here, intended to help protect areas of critical concern for conservation and research.

DO NOT REMOVE ARTIFACTS OR FOSSILS: It's illegal, disrespectful, and ruins the experience for others. Even moving potsherds can hinder the researcher's ability to properly document and study the site.

LOOK BUT DON'T TOUCH: Touching rock art, artifacts, historic and prehistoric structures, or fossils can speed up the deterioration, and can accidentally break or destroy them. Never alter or remove any rock art and do not grind anything in grinding stones or slicks.

PACK IT IN, (PICK IT UP), PACK IT OUT: Always haul out any trash or waste that you bring or create on your hikes.

POOP ETHICS: It happens. Deal with it properly in the backcountry by always doing your duty away from water sources and the trail. Dig a small cathole at least 6 inches deep and bury your crap. In select areas, Park Service–issued waste disposal bags are required.

HISTORIC TRASH IS NOT TRASH: Beyond obvious trash (like food wrappers and camping equipment), things that appear to be trash like old rusty tin cans and broken bottles can provide clues about the historic period for researchers. Do not touch these items; it is illegal to remove anything over fifty years old.

THIS IS NOT YOUR HOUSE: Do not camp, start fires, eat, or go to the bathroom in or near archaeological remains. All can potentially cause damage, plus it's rude—no one invited you over!

STAY CAIRN-FREE: Please do not build new cairns (rock towers marking trails). While you are likely to encounter cairns along many hikes, no additional cairns are needed to litter the landscape and view. Cairns made by hikers instead of land managers are often incorrect and can lead you astray (be careful).

SIGN IN AND PAY UP: Signing the trail register and filling out a permit helps the BLM track low-impact recreation numbers, which directly factors into future land management planning. Paying permits and use fees help with monitoring and enforcement, as well as amenities like toilets.

CHECK FIRE REGULATIONS: These can vary in each area and during different times of year. Always use either a fire pan or pre-existing fire rings (except those within prehistoric and historic sites). Always completely extinguish the embers.

DON'T BUST THE CRUST: Please stay on pre-existing trails and off the delicate and living cryptobiotic soil—the dark brown or black clumps on the surface of sand. Besides, smashing cryptocrust and increasing erosion is the job of the BLM-permitted cattle.

SOCIAL MEDIA: It's natural to want to share photos from your trip on social media, but please refrain from referencing locations and GPS points for sensitive sites. While all routes and sites in this book are publicly available, it is best to let future explorers do their own research to guide their trip.

DRIVE ON OFFICIAL ROADS: Always drive on existing roads to prevent damage to the landscape and cultural sites.

WRITE YOUR HEART OUT: If you love Grand Staircase-Escalante and care about its future, write it a love letter, or more specifically a letter to the BLM and elected congressional officials voicing your concerns and ideas. Public input is always accepted and considered for future land management planning, and now more than ever it is critical for the public to speak up. While it's natural to want to write from the heart, the more specific and rooted in concrete details and references your letter is, the more likely it is to be taken into consideration by the BLM and Congress. Regardless of your political leanings, this is a truly American privilege to be a part of how YOUR public lands are managed and what their future looks like.

You Could Die Out Here

Anything that lives in the desert must be passionately devoted to its own survival. The plants and animals (and people) who thrive in these conditions all have developed unique adaptations to survive dangerous conditions—including their own ways to fight back. You however, eager hiker, are not one of these creatures. The desert will not hesitate to kill you if you are unprepared or unaware. The following is a run-down of the primary suspects in the Grand Staircase-Escalante murder-mob.

DEHYDRATION AND HEAT EXHAUSTION

While Grand Staircase-Escalante National Monument holds considerable water sources, it is still the desert, and much of the terrain you hike through will be barren, exposed, and HOT!

To prevent heatstroke and dehydration, stay well hydrated. Always carry plenty of water, bring a water filter or water treatment, and know how to find water sources on each route. Enhance your water with an electrolyte supplement to prevent hyponatremia (drinking too much plain water can actually dilute sodium levels in your bloodstream, which can also be deadly). Use sunscreen and reapply often, seek shade frequently to cool off, start early in the day when temperatures are cooler, pace yourself (starting slowly will prevent over-exertion and overheating), and dunk articles of clothing in cool water to lower core body temperature. Always pay attention to your vitals and other signs of heatstroke: rapid heart rate, loss of sweating, red skin, throbbing headache, dizziness, rapid shallow breathing, disorientation, seizures, and unconsciousness.

Don't become a bleached set of bones!

HYPOTHERMIA

Don't laugh—freezing to death (hypothermia) is one of the most common causes of death in the desert. Major contrasts between daytime highs and nighttime lows, paired with frequent cold pools of water and/or water crossings, make this a year-round threat, especially for hikers who are not prepared with dry layers. Snow is possible even in the lower elevations during winter. Keep the following in mind to prevent hypothermia and frostbite: wear plenty of warm layers and specifically protect your head, hands, feet, and toes, as these areas lose heat the quickest and are also most susceptible to

Desert ice.

damage from the cold; stay hydrated (this can seem less important when it is very cold outside, but drinking water or a sports drink with electrolytes will help your body regulate its temperature); and stay dry (have extra layers with you and keep snow out of your boots). Lastly, pay attention to the following symptoms and seek help should they surface: redness and a stinging, burning, throbbing, or prickling sensation followed by numbness.

FLASH FLOODING

Flash flooding is always a threat in canyon country and applies to nearly every route in this guide. The canyons themselves were formed by the passage of water eroding their walls, and serving as drainage points for rainwater. Monsoon season (roughly July to September) is the peak of danger when daily thunderstorms can drop several inches of water in minutes over a relatively small area resulting in several feet of powerful rushing water downcanyon. While it is wise to avoid entering a canyon when storm clouds are present overhead (or distant), on a perfectly sunny day, a storm 50 miles away can fill a dry canyon with rushing water, destroying everything in its path! It most likely will start with a bit of running water and quickly build in surges into a massive maelstrom.

To avoid this desert phenomenon, travel to these areas during the peak seasons of spring (late April to May) or fall (September and October). Regardless of the time of year, be prepared and remain aware of the weather. If thunderstorms are forecast, you see storm clouds forming, or hear thunder and/or see lightning in the distance do not enter the canyons.

If you find yourself caught in a canyon during a storm or flash flood, seek higher ground immediately! A good rule of thumb is to go twice as high as you feel you need to be to avoid the rushing water. A better rule is to get the hell out of the canyon. Observe closely the watermarks along canyon walls from previous flooding. If you are camping in a canyon, be sure to set up above the watermark, preferably with a safe path to move to higher ground or escape if needed.

NAVIGATION

Most of the routes included in this guidebook are NOT marked and require self-navigation. In Wilderness Areas, trails are usually NOT maintained. Cairns can be misleading, and often there will be no one else on the routes to ask for directions (to the extent you dare trust the knowledge of strangers). In addition to this guidebook, hikers must carry and know how to use a compass and a topo map. Map suggestions are provided for each route based on pre-monument regions. When considering use of GPS or a smart phone with a fancy map app, please understand their limitations in an area without cell service and with longer routes that will often outlast a typical device battery.

TECHNICAL AND TREACHEROUS TERRAIN

The hikes described in this guidebook may not be technical canyoneering, but they are still teeming with terrain that will test you and your safety. Scrambling and down climbing are common, and a simple misstep on a slippery boulder during a creek crossing can pose a hidden threat. Other perils include cliffs, slickrock slabs and ledges, high exposure, boulder fields, thick thorny brush, fallen trees, uneven rocky ground, baby heads (melon-sized rounded boulders in creek beds), hidden slot canyons, cacti, quicksand, slick mud, water crossings, pour-overs, dryfalls, sand, and more often than not, a combination of all of these obstacles at once.

Slot canyons are an especially important landscape feature to consider as several routes mentioned in this book feature points of no return (the only way out is through) or are significantly harder to approach if a turnaround is needed.

Read the route descriptions carefully and do not attempt any routes featuring terrain that you are not experienced and comfortable with. For those unaccustomed to desert terrain, specifically in southeastern Utah, there are plenty of easy dayhikes to practice on. If you attempt moderate to difficult hikes, always do so prepared and with the mindset to confront each "obstacle" with a calculated and controlled attitude, and be ready to retreat if any terrain proves too dangerous or you are uncertain that you can proceed safely.

COMMUNICATION IN REMOTE AREAS

Before heading out into remote backcountry areas, always let somebody know where you are going and when you plan to return. Signing the trail register also helps track your general whereabouts. It is recommended that you carry a satellite device to call for help in case of an emergency. In tight canyons this may not always be effective. Bring a signal mirror as a back up. Due to the remote nature of these areas, help will likely not arrive quickly, so always be prepared with a first aid kit and as much safety and survival gear—plus knowledge—as possible. You (and hopefully at least one hiking partner) are the first responder to your survival needs.

Summer is rattlesnake season and it is best to keep calm, and your distance, when encountering these venomous reptilia. If you or your hiking partner does get bit, remove any restrictive clothing/shoes/jewelry near the bite and keep it lower than heart level. Seek medical attention immediately.

The area is home to black widow and hobo spiders—both are poisonous to humans and nocturnal, making them a bigger threat at your campsite than on your hike. If that scares you, that's what tents are for! If you do get bit by a black widow, clean the area with soap and water before applying antiseptic. Cover with a cold compress and elevate the area, then quickly seek medical attention. Hobos are found hiding out in wood or rock piles and fields, and take the same precautions as with black widows if you get bit. Pay special attention for signs of dizziness, numbness, or blistering at the site of the bite.

While most scorpions rate on a danger scale equivalent with bee stings, an injection of venom by the Arizona Bark Scor-

pion (found in south-central Utah) can be fatal. If you are bit, seek medical attention immediately and if possible go straight to an emergency room or call 911. Also be sure to clean the area and apply a cool compress (alternating 10 minutes on and 10 minutes off).

POISON IVY

No, poison ivy won't kill you but you might wish you were dead if your skin reacts to the oils found in this unpleasant plant. Look out for green (and occasionally red) teardrop-shaped leaves in clusters of three per branch. Death Hollow is notoriously filled with this species, but be on the lookout for it throughout the monument, especially in areas near constant water sources.

YOURSELF

The desert is a place that requires self-reliance. The opportunities for you to make a dangerous or deadly mistake are numerous, while the bailout options and options for help are few. You are your own first line of defense to avoid the hazards outlined in this chapter, so keen observation and responsible decision-making are your choice weapons. Remember, no hike is worth risking your life.

Permits and Ranger Stations

Most overnight routes listed in this guidebook require a permit, which fortunately are often available for free directly at the trailhead. This is especially important not only as a safety measure, but also because the BLM uses them as a measurement of low-impact recreation. These stats factor into multiuse policies, management decisions and, as discussed earlier, as a way to more designated Wilderness.

Permits and information are also available at the BLM field offices and visitor centers listed here. Of particular interest to you will be hiking and road conditions, which often change daily in this area. The offices are all managed under varying, confusing, and inconvenient seasonal hours, so do your homework ahead of time. The other option is to just do your own homework—talk to locals at the coffee shop, take note of the actual weather outside, and use this guidebook!

Please note that several routes fall outside the boundaries of Grand Staircase-Escalante National Monument (BLM management) and within the bounds of Glen Canyon National Recreation Area, which is managed by the Park Service. Permits are also available at most trailheads, but these areas are subject to a more extensive

Vote with your feet—sign the trail register.

list of rules and the oversight of park rangers. In addition to checking permits, rangers are enforcers of the requirement to bring, use, and haul out a Park Service–issued waste bag for your poop on popular hikes like Coyote Gulch.

Grand Staircase-Escalante National Monument

It doesn't exactly roll off the tongue, but the long-winded name seems to fit the expanse of this place. Originally designated at almost two million acres, it was larger than Delaware, and over fifty times larger than its neighboring Bryce Canyon National Park. But those that focus on the size of manmade lines on a map seem to be missing the point, as GSENM is part of a larger geography. From the Grand Canyon and Vermillion Cliffs to the south, to the Paunsaugunt and Aquarius Plateaus to the north, the Grand Staircase encompasses a greater landscape that connects a vast wilderness that includes Grand Canyon National Park, Zion National Park, Bryce Canyon National Park, the Grand Staircase, the Kaiparowits Plateau, Canyons of the Escalante, Glen Canyon, Capitol Reef National Park, Cedar Mesa and Bears Ears, San Rafael Swell, Canyonlands National Park, and even across the Four Corners, well into the Navajo Nation and the San Juan River watershed in Colorado.

GEOGRAPHY OF GSENM

The greater Grand Staircase-Escalante area encompasses three distinct regions: the **Grand Staircase** and Paria Watershed bordering Bryce and Zion Canyon to the west; the **Kaiparowits Plateau** bordering the Vermillion Cliffs to the south and Glen Canyon to the east; and the **Canyons of the Escalante** watershed bordering Glen Canyon and Capitol Reef to the northeast.

THE GRAND STAIRCASE

Geologist Clarence Dutton first described this area in the 1870s as a staircase ascending the older sedimentary rock layers of the Grand Canyon, all the way to the younger Pink Cliffs of Cedar Breaks and Bryce Canyon. Similar in concept to C. Hart Merriam's life zones based on elevation and precipitation, the Grand Staircase ascends the walls of the Grand Canyon to the Kaibab Plateau, and continues climbing up in elevation via a series of cliff bands and plateaus. Interestingly, these bands of sedimentary layers are exposed and easy to locate and identify, interconnected by its complimentary plateaus, giving arise to the staircase comparison. The series of cliffs from lower elevation to higher, and in a general south to north direction are as follows:

1. Grand Canyon
    (not always included in Grand Staircase descriptions)
2. Chocolate Cliffs
3. Vermillion Cliffs
4. White Cliffs
5. Gray Cliffs
6. Pink Cliffs

We encourage readers to create clever mnemonic devices to remember these bands, such as

"Gee Chuck, Chino Valley Was a Good Place."

The Grand Staircase coupled with Merriam's life zone concept do well in generally describing both the geography and natural history of the Southwest, and how the two are interrelated and dependent upon one another.

KAIPAROWITS PLATEAU

This huge elevated plateau covers nearly 1,700 square miles between the Paria and Escalante rivers. Few roads cut through the expanse, and the BLM has designated a large patchwork of Wilderness Areas on and around the plateau. As a result, the Kaiparowits remains one of the last wild places in the Lower 48, and as such provides unique research opportunities for archaeology, paleontology, botany, and natural history as well as unique opportunities for backcountry low-impact recreation.

On the northeast edge lie the Straight Cliffs, a nearly 50-mile unbroken chain of mostly sandstone cliffs parallel to Hole-In-The-Rock Road and the Escalante River. The southern section is cut by a number of water drainages eventually ending in Lake Powell, including the Burning Hills Wilderness Study Area.

The plateau runs from about 4,000 feet in elevation to almost 8,000 feet at its highest northerly end. The landscape is largely piñon and juniper transitioning into the higher ecotones of ponderosa pine and even montane forests of fur, spruce and aspen at its highest reaches.

The plateau contains large tracts of coal, especially on the southern end, which has been left out of the new monument boundaries after President Trump's 2017 executive order.

CANYONS OF THE ESCALANTE

The watershed of the Escalante River includes the endless terrain of side drainages, slot canyons, and tributaries of a large expanse of wilderness, including the Box Death Hollow Wilderness, Capitol Reef, and Glen Canyon. It is here, more than

A packraft hiking down the Escalante River.

any other area in the monument, that recreation is the major player. The high volume of water in the area creates sprawling networks of slot canyons, natural bridges, arches, waterfalls, sand dunes, and unique geological features.

The Glen Canyon groups of sandstones dominate the exposed rock within the watershed, including Navajo, Entrada, and Wingate sandstones.

The river now joins the flooded Glen Canyon at Lake Powell via the Escalante Arm.

National Monument Status

GSENM's expanse is overwhelming, hard to fathom, hard to know. For decades, GSENM, along with Bears Ears, represented a blank spot on our maps. Popularly touted as "the last place in the Lower 48 to be mapped," it is a wild, expansive "oasis" of wilderness that in one way or another has always been under the microscope, either for conservation or resource exploitation.

In the 1930s, Secretary of the Interior Harold Ickes proposed the 4.5-million-acre Escalante National Monument,

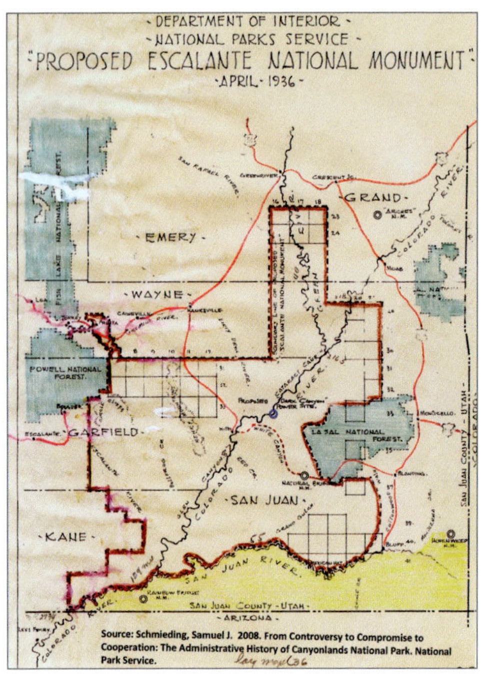

Original map for 1936 Proposed Escalante NM.

including areas of Canyonlands, Glen Canyon, Escalante, Grand Staircase, Capitol Reef, and Bears Ears. The initiative was on track to be approved by the President, and was only interrupted and eventually abandoned due to the eruption of World War II. It's hard to imagine the landscape, both literally (think no dam) and metaphorically, if the Escalante National Monument had been established way back in 1936.

The initiative was partially fulfilled with the eventual declaration of Canyonlands and Capitol Reef National Parks, Box Death Hollow Wilderness, Glen Canyon National Recreation Area, then finally in the 1990s with the declaration of GSENM, and in 2016 when President Obama declared Bears Ears a National Monument.

In 2017, President Trump signed an executive order reducing GSENM by roughly 50 percent and Bears Ears by 85 percent. The order split Grand Staircase into three national monuments, reflecting the geography of the region—**Grand Staircase National Monument, Kaiparowits National Monument, and Canyons of the Escalante National Monument**. Notably absent from the new monuments were the large tracts of land that contain access roads and coal deposits.

Following the reduction, lawsuits were filed by environmental and tribal organizations fighting the executive order to reduce both Grand Staircase-Escalante and Bears Ears National Monuments. The lawsuits stated that the president does not have the authority to reduce or repeal previously declared national monuments and that doing so is a violation of the Antiquities Act. On October 8, 2021, President Biden used the Antiquities Act to restore Grand Staircase-Escalante National Monument in its entirety, 1.88 million acres, along with Bears Ears.

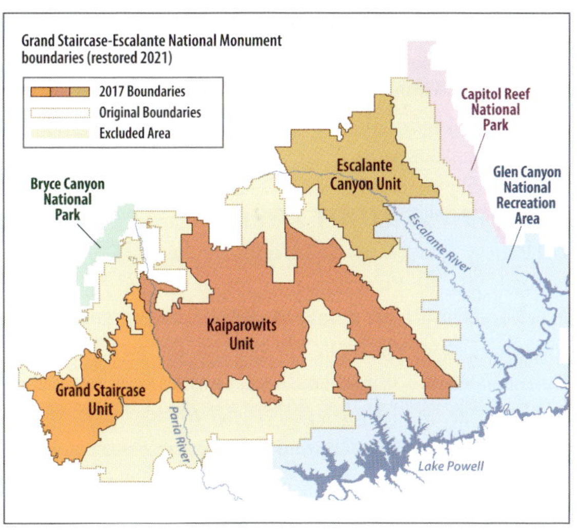

AMERICA'S RED ROCKS WILDERNESS ACT

Fortunately for both Grand Staircase-Escalante and Bears Ears, much of the lands within their boundaries are declared Wilderness Areas or Wilderness Study Areas (WSAs). Both Wilderness Areas and WSAs actually offer *more* protections than monument status, but lack the funding support to manage and enforce rules that would come with monument status. A conversion of all WSAs to declared Wilderness, and the inclusion of applicable unprotected lands to be determined as Wilderness has long been a goal, the Holy Grail if you will, of wilderness conservation groups and activists in southern Utah.

Enter America's Red Rock Wilderness Act. Introduced to the House every year since 1989, this audacious bill would do just that. Including not just Bears Ears and Grand Staircase, but other important areas, the bill would radically change public land management in southern Utah, as well as offer up the highest level of protections via Wilderness status, to the many areas now under threat from developers. While the act requires an act of Congress, which is much more difficult than getting a President to sign off on a National Monument, if passed it would protect these areas legally and irreversibly, no matter who holds the throne of POTUS.

For more information visit the Southern Utah Wilderness Alliance (suwa.org).

WILDERNESS STUDY AREAS

Wilderness Study Areas are defined by the BLM to be areas of land that fit the criteria to be considered Wilderness Areas, and as such are managed appropriately to maintain its wilderness character. While WSAs enjoy the protections and management of a Wilderness Area, Congress has not passed legislation declaring these areas officially Wilderness.

America's Red Rock bill would effectively convert all WSAs to designated Wilderness, as well as lands previously within the National Monuments that are no longer protected by either Monument or WSA status.

The following is a list of WSAs within GSENM that await Wilderness designation.

Carcass Canyon WSA

The Blues WSA

Death Ridge WSA

Burning Hills WSA

Wahweap WSA

Fiftymile Mountain WSA

Paria-Hackberry WSA

Mud Spring Canyon WSA

Devil's Garden WSA

Phipps-Death Hollow WSA

North Escalante Canyons/The Gulch WSA

Steep Creek WSA

The Cockscomb WSA

Scorpion WSA

Scorpion 2 WSA

Escalante Canyons Tract 5 WSA

THE RESEARCH MONUMENT

"The Grand Staircase-Escalante National Monument's vast and austere landscape embraces a spectacular array of scientific and historic resources. This high, rugged, and remote region, where bold plateaus and multi-hued cliffs run for distances that defy human perspective, was the last place in the continental United States to be mapped. Even today, this unspoiled natural area remains a frontier, a quality that greatly enhances the monument's value for scientific study. The monument has a long and dignified human history: it is a place where one can see how nature shapes human endeavors in the American West, where distance and aridity have been pitted against our dreams and courage. The monument presents exemplary opportunities for geologists, paleontologists, archeologists, historians, and biologists." (Proclamation 6920—Establishment of the Grand Staircase-Escalante National Monument)

President Clinton's 1996 Proclamation eloquently explains the groundbreaking research opportunities as the purpose and priority for protecting its 1.8 million acres. Major discoveries have and continue to be made in the fields of paleontology and geology in what is often described as a massive outdoor laboratory. The area's human history is rich and varied. It is home to tremendous plant and wildlife, with many endemic and endangered species. The protection and conservation of the greater Grand Staircase region is imperative to future study that will continue to push the boundaries of what we know, not just about this swath of southern Utah, but also about our planet's past, present, and future. With the restoration of Grand Staircase comes a renewed opportunity to fulfill its scientific research potential, which has been stymied by reduction of funds, political pressure, and the previous reduction.

PALEONTOLOGY

The Grand Staircase preserves one of the most continuous and detailed records of terrestrial vertebrate evolution between 98 and 73 million years ago, thanks to the abundant Late

Cretaceous rocks, according to Katja Knoll, Paleontology Lab Manager for the Grand Staircase Partners, who provided the content for this section. She explains, "The well-preserved fossil material found in the Kaiparowits Plateau region of GSENM allows for a detailed glimpse into the unique paleo-ecosystem of the southern part of Laramidia, the island continent that once stretched from Alaska to Mexico. The sedimentary rocks of the Kaiparowits Plateau region represent a unique ecosystem unknown anywhere else in North America during that time. Many animals discovered from this region are morphologically distinct and part of a whole new ecosystem, and these discoveries are continuously changing our understanding of terrestrial vertebrate evolution of this time period. There are few places on this planet that provide a window into this important time, so the Late Cretaceous rocks of the Kaiparowits Plateau have quickly become a very important scientific resource."

At least thirty new species of dinosaurs have been unearthed (thirteen have been officially named) from GSENM, with twenty found on the Kaiparowits Formation. Other notable paleontological discoveries within GSENM include:

- Oldest known diagnostic centrosaurine ceratopsid, called *Diabloceratops eatoni*
- Oldest known true tyrannosaurid, *Lythronax argestes*
- Highest Late Campanian ceratopsid diversity
- Oldest diagnostic mosasaur specimen from North America from the marine Tropic Shale Formation
- One of the oldest North American ankylosaurids
- Southern USA's best preserved tyrannosaur
- Southern USA's only known mass tyrannosaur burial site
- Largest Campanian age oviraptorid dinosaur species (*Hagryphus giganteus*)
- Highest diversity of late Campanian fossil flora known

GEOLOGY

The monument's name literally denotes the geological layers for which this swath of the Colorado Plateau is built upon. "These layers of sedimentary rock reflect ever-changing environments as a result of tectonic shifts, sea level fluctuations and changing global climate. These rocks range in age from the middle Permian (approx. 270 million years ago) to the Late Cretaceous (approx. 74 million years ago). Most of the rocks exposed in both the Grand Staircase and the Canyons of the Escalante regions are of Triassic and Jurassic age, whereas the sedimentary rocks of the Kaiparowits Plateau date back primarily to the Late Cretaceous." (Knoll)

From housing the plethora of fossils being unearthed within the Monument, enriching the very specific mineral composition of the soil that makes plant and animal life possible, to the unique erodibility that makes the formation of canyons possible, ROCK is the heart of Grand Staircase-Escalante.

But even rock forged over millions of years is vulnerable in the hands of man. These layers contain mineral resources including coal, oil, gas, copper, and other minerals that have not been heavily extracted due to the remoteness of their locations, inefficiency of extraction, and resulting low value, and up until now the protection as a National Monument has prevented new mining/leasing activity since 1996. Following the reduction of the monument, a proposed copper mine is already being explored near the Circle Cliffs (which were already exploited in their previous pre-monument life by oil and gas extraction). The Kaiparowits Plateau, the high-density site for paleontological and archaeological research, is also the location of rich coal deposits (the Burning Hills) with whispers of future development looming like a constant shadow.

Nearly the entire landscape here is a geological wonder worthy of landmark status, and many unique geological features and major discoveries have been unearthed in GSENM. The Wolverine Petrified Forest (within the Circle Cliffs) is the location of one of the largest petrified forests in North America.

Only rock is real. — Edward Abbey

The study of these past trees show that GSENM was a tropical rainforest long before it became desert! Moqui Marbles (also known as Martian Blueberries) are sandstone balls encapsulated in iron derived from groundwater. These formations have been found in GSENM and on Mars, providing evidence for water on the red planet at one time. The area is rumored to have nearly as many arches as Arches National Park, including many that were left out of the monument boundaries. (Jeff Moore, Associate Professor of Geology and Geophysics at the University of Utah)

ARCHAEOLOGY

Serious archaeological research did not begin in the Grand Staircase region until the 1920's, and remained scattered until more substantive study began with the 1996 monument designation. Since that time over 5,000 new archaeological sites have been discovered within the monument. (Grand Staircase Partners; gsenm.org/get-the-facts/)

Archaeologist R.E. Burrillo, whose research specializes in the Grand Staircase region, describes the human prehistory of this area for the *Archaeological Record*:

The first people to permeate the greater Southwest were Paleoindian foragers dating back to the late Pleistocene (Ice Age) era. Climate change at the end of that era caused many of the big game animals on which people were dependent to broaden their diets, with broadened sociocultural practices following suit. This was the Archaic period, during which foragers developed elaborate basketry and began using grinding stones for small food items like seeds. Although rare, Archaic rock art panels in the GSENM area are among the most astounding. The end of the Archaic period was signaled by the arrival of corn agriculture, and the early Basketmaker—or Basketmaker II—period saw people living in semi-sedentary homes. Basketmaker II archaeology is not especially well known in the GSENM area; but the succeeding Basketmaker III period, with its ceramics and bow-and-arrow technology, can be found throughout the Grand Staircase. Subsequent occupation by Ancestral Pueblo peoples during the Pueblo I and II periods is also concentrated primarily in the Staircase, although the last era—late PII to early PIII—saw occupation by Pueblo peoples in the Kaiparowits area as far up as Boulder. Meanwhile, a day's walk to the east, the Fremont culture occupied the Escalante drainage during the bulk of the Ancestral Pueblo period. Although also practicing corn agriculture, the Fremont were much more mobile and seasonal, and in the GSENM area they also created some of the most exquisite rock art. Whether or not the two groups had any sort of quantifiable relationship is an ongoing question, but both of them were gone from the area by the mid-1200s.

The first hikers in the region were nomadic foragers.

By the time Euro-Americans had infiltrated the area, it had become fully occupied by several bands of the Numic-speaking Ute/Paiute culture, who migrated into it from the west. Like the earliest occupants of the region, they eschewed agriculture in favor of being foragers. Euro-American settlement hadn't fully saturated the GSENM area until the establishment of Escalante in 1875, starting point of the famous Hole-in-the-Rock Expedition that tethers GSENM to Bears Ears in the chronicles of Mormon history. With Euro-Americans came grazing, and with grazing came changes to the local environment that made it all but impossible for the Paiutes—or anybody else—to draw a sustainable living from wild resources in the area. Subsequent grazing, mining, and even logging took their respective tolls on the fragile ecosystems of the GSENM area through the historic and early modern era, until the monument designation put a halt to their expansion. Nowadays the primary cash crops of the area are science and recreation, even while more destructive forces once again take aim…

Datura meteloides:
Moonflower.

NATURAL SCIENCE

Flora (Plants)

The Grand Staircase-Escalante region is the richest floristic region in the Intermountain West (with three major floras meeting here) and is home to nearly 85% of Utah's plant life (over 900 species) and 50% (174 species) of the state's endemic plants. It is also important to note that Utah as a whole has arguably one of the highest rates of endemic plants in the U.S. The unique mineral composition of the area's soils creates an environment that fosters only plants uniquely suited to thrive in this harsh environment. For example, eleven known species within Grand Staircase are found nowhere else on the planet. The continued relative isolation of the region and relative lack of roads has largely protected it from invasive species (with major exceptions including Russian olive and tamarisk that have taken over the Escalante Watershed thanks to human introduction). The largest threats to plant life within the monument are cattle grazing, road construction, urbanization, mining, OHVs and other forms of human development, which are increasing in relevance under the current monument reductions.

Fauna (Animals)

The variety of life zones (with elevations ranging from 4,500 to 9,000 feet), flourishing and varied plant species, and abundant water sources create the foundation for surprisingly high levels of biodiversity. Over 2,600 species live within Grand Staircase-Escalante National Monument. Hailing back to their direct dinosaur ancestors, 200 bird species flourish within the monument, twenty of which are raptors, and notably including the endangered California condor and threatened bald eagle. Reptiles and amphibians abound, with the native desert night lizard and chuckwalla both listed as sensitive species. The range of biomes make the Grand Staircase region a welcoming home for many mammals with high concentrations of bats, bighorn sheep, pack rats, mule deer and even mountain lions in the higher elevation terrain. Finally, any mention of the beehive state surely needs to mention its namesake—fittingly, 648 species of bees can be found buzzing around this monument.

A band of bighorn sheep observe a strange blonde animal running by.

Regional Overview

It is impossible to cover 1.8 million acres of some of the most treacherously captivating terrain in one lifetime. To encapsulate, summarize, and condense into one guidebook is an even sillier proposition. Below is a rough overview and gross underrepresentation of the regional zones and major features of the greater Grand Staircase region.

AQUARIUS PLATEAU

The highest timbered plateau in North America, the Aquarius Plateau is 100 miles long on the north edge of the Grand Staircase (900 square miles). This plateau (accessed via Hwy. 12) is diversely forested with aspen, spruce, fir, and sub-alpine grasslands at high elevations; ponderosas at middle elevations; and juniper grow throughout its lower reaches. The Aquarius borders Bryce Canyon National Park, overlooks GSENM and Capitol Reef National Park, and includes the Box Death Hollow Wilderness.

BRYCE CANYON NATIONAL PARK

Comprising much of the pink cliffs of the Grand Staircase, Bryce Canyon National Park features the largest collection of hoodoos in the world. The park has an elevation of 6–9,000 feet and is best known for hiking and scenic drives.

CAPITOL REEF NATIONAL PARK

Bordering the northern edge of Grand Staircase-Escalante National Monument and Glen Canyon National Recreation Area, Capitol Reef is teeming with geological formations (cliffs, domes, arches, monoliths) and is a part of a 100-mile waterpocket fold (monocline) that's 65 million years old. Many of the rock formations are white Navajo Sandstone (and thus the "Capitol" refers to the look of many domes resembling state capitol buildings). Reef is a local word meaning any rocky barrier that impedes travel. The monument is frequented primarily for hiking and scenic drives. The park is approximately 60 miles long and 6 miles wide. It can be accessed from Grand Staircase-Escalante National Monument via the Burr Trail.

CIRCLE CLIFFS (WOLVERINE LOOP)

Circle Cliffs

The Circle Cliffs and surrounding canyons are notable for their Wingate Sandstone composition (most of the surrounding sandstone is the much softer Navajo formation). Amongst the cliffs are two standout GSENM attractions: Wolverine Canyon (that features a petrified forest) and Little Death Hollow. The Circle Cliffs and nearby hiking routes are most commonly accessed via the Burr Trail and the adjacent Wolverine Loop. Portions of this zone have been removed from National Monument boundaries and a proposed copper mine is being explored as of 2018.

ESCALANTE RIVER

Escalante River

Part of GSENM and National Conservation Lands, the Escalante River is a tributary of the Colorado River ending at Glen Canyon (Lake Powell), flowing southeast from the town of Escalante for approximately 90 miles. The river corridor passes through many sandstone gorges and offers numerous hiking possibilities (and is a great water source for many routes in this book). Although the flow is often quite low with an average of less than 150 cfs, it can still be a popular route for packrafts and stand-up paddle boards during higher runoff (spring snowmelt/runoff and late summer monsoon season).

GLEN CANYON NATIONAL RECREATION AREA

Constructed between 1959 and 1966, the Glen Canyon Dam is one of the largest man-made dams in the U.S. (710 feet) and diverts water from the Colorado River to provide water and hydroelectric power for millions of people in the West. The controversial project effectively changed the landscape from a flowing river between towering red sandstone canyons to a lake with 1,960 miles of shoreline and a capacity to store over 26 million acre feet of water (in what is now Lake Powell). The water levels began rising in 1963 and continued to rise until 1980, slowly drowning the area's rich archaeological, ecological, and geological wonders while radically changing the surrounding landscape. Glen Canyon also encapsulates the popular Colorado River put-in site of Lee's Ferry, which sits at the Paria River/Colorado River confluence. Lee's Ferry borders the Vermillion Cliffs, sits several miles downriver from the Glen Canyon Dam, and is the official beginning of Grand Canyon National Park.

KAIPAROWITS PLATEAU

The Kaiparowits is one of the most remote, wild, and rugged places in the western U.S., standing at upwards of 7,500 feet elevation. Its northeastern boundary, the Straight Cliffs (paralleling Hole-In-The-Rock Road), was once an ancient shoreline. Smoky Mountain Road provides the main human access to the plateau, connecting Escalante with its southern reaches near Lake Powell and Big Water via a 78-mile 4WD road. The isolation of the Kaiparowits enhances its wild qualities, making it an ideal home to an exceptional variety of plant life. The plateau is well known to contain unique fossil remains in its sandstone layers and an abundance of dinosaur fossils. There are 300 known archaeological sites within the plateau, which provide unique insight to human prehistory in the region. The Burning Hills—literally naturally burning underground coal beds—are a visual reminder that this special place is home to plentiful natural resources, making its preservation as a Wilderness of utmost importance to protect its unique valuable natural state from resource extraction.

ESCALANTE CANYONS

While narrow and slotted canyons are prevalent throughout Grand Staircase-Escalante and the greater Colorado Plateau, the Escalante Canyons region (north of Escalante and primarily off of Hole-In-The-Rock Road) is a high-density hotspot for these water-worn passageways through the earth. Sections of uniform rock (mainly Navajo Sandstone in this area) are whittled away somewhat evenly by the forces of flowing water (from creeks, rainfall and monsoons) and filled with debris (sand, small stones and even wood). For most, the Escalante Canyons will be the primary attraction in Grand Staircase-Escalante National Monument.

THE COCKSCOMB

Bisecting the heart of Grand Staircase-Escalante National Monument (and beyond toward the Grand Canyon), The Cockscomb East Kaibab Monocline is a 100-mile long sedimentary rock ridgeline formed by uplift and erosion. Cottonwood Canyon Road parallels the Cockscomb.

PARIA RIVER

This 95-mile tributary of the Colorado River flows through Grand Staircase-Escalante National Monument and the Vermillion Cliffs National Monument until it joins with the

Colorado in Grand Canyon National Park at Lee's Ferry. The lower stretch of the Paria flows through a beautiful narrow canyon (the Paria Narrows) and can be linked with Buckskin Gulch (dubbed "the longest slot canyon in the world"). Several past human settlers have made their

homes near the Paria River as evidenced by nearby archaeological sites and the ghost town of Pareah. Several western films were made at a riverside movie set that burned to the ground in 2006.

VERMILLION CLIFFS NATIONAL MONUMENT

Sitting on the Arizona side of the Utah/Arizona border, Vermillion Cliffs National Monument encompasses 294,000 acres of public land adjacent to Grand Staircase-Escalante National Monument. The monument includes Paria Canyon, much of Buckskin Gulch (listed in this guidebook), The Wave (one of the most difficult rock formations to see thanks to a stringent permit lottery system), and Coyote Buttes.

GRAND CANYON NATIONAL PARK

Known the world over simply as the "Grand Canyon," the massive canyon, over one mile deep, has been forged by the Colorado River for over 6 million years, and the river now flows through its divide over the course of 277 river miles. The canyon is prized for its beauty and is layered in geological, ecological, historical, and cultural value. Despite its protected status as a National Park, areas surrounding the Grand Canyon face significant threats from human development including a proposed tramway to the bottom of the canyon and eager Uranium miners.

Town Of Escalante By David Roberts
(Excerpted from *Escalante's Dream*)

In 1875, Almon H. Thompson, a government geographer who was John Wesley Powell's brother-in-law, undertook a vast pioneering survey of some of the ruggedest country in southern Utah, including the Henry Mountains, the Aquarius Plateau, and the Kaiparowits Plateau. Coming down from Fifty-Mile Mountain (as the locals called Kaiparowits) in early August, he ran into a group of Mormons from Panguitch who were starting to lay out a town on the banks of the river that bisects this desert-like outback. Those settlers were hoping that a town at a lower elevation than Panguitch would provide a longer growing season. They had tentatively named the new settlement Potato Valley.

Thompson struck up a conversation with these hardy pilgrims. In his diary entry for August 5, he wrote, "Saw four Mormons from Panguitch who were talking about making a settlement here. Advised them to call the place Escalante." No doubt Thompson filled in the men about the glorious failure the expedition led by two Franciscan priests out of Santa Fe had prosecuted a century earlier. The locals liked the idea, and slapped the name of Escalante on the fledgling settlement.

Thompson was already referring to the river as the Escalante, even though its discoverer had called it Birch Creek. Thompson's team thus honored the padre because the river's mouth "was not a great distance up from where Escalante had crossed the Colorado." In any event, it's clear that the architects of Potato Valley knew nothing about the Domínguez-Escalante expedition until they consulted with Thompson.

Jump ahead 48 years. In 1923, a sociologist named Lowry Nelson came to Escalante, intent on including the town in his study of Mormon villages. He found that the locals uniformly pronounced the name "Es-ca-LANT," rhyming it with "slant" and rendering the Spanish final "e" silent. Just so the citizens pronounce the name today. When Nelson asked his informants about the origin of the name, they said that it was an old Indian word whose meaning had been lost.

A Roadside Guide to GSENM

Though your love for hiking may be great, the way to the heart of Grand Staircase-Escalante is undoubtedly through its arterial network of (mostly) dirt roads. With the exception of paved Highway 89 and Highway 12, many of the hikes in this guidebook are accessed via dirt roads, primarily Hole-In-The-Rock Road (essentially the "Main Drag") and Cottonwood Canyon Road. Additional hikes are found off of Skutumpah Road and Burr Trail Road. Bikepacking is increasing in popularity around the monument and is a viable way to commute to your hiking destinations while keeping your adventures completely human powered.

A NOTE ON ROADS IN GSENM: The quality of many of the roads in GSENM and in greater southern Utah can vary greatly depending on the weather. The dirt roads mentioned here are well maintained year-round, and in dry season are passable by a medium clearance 2WD vehicle and able driver. However, during wet weather the upper layer of clay can turn the road into a slip-and-slide, and is not recommended even for 4WD vehicles. Plan accordingly, as there are no services and no tow trucks to come save you.

MAJOR ROADS

Hole-In-The-Rock Road

This byway is named for the Mormon settlers who decided to blast a hole in the canyon walls near the Colorado River to ultimately settle the town of Bluff, Utah. Only remnants of the actual "hole" remain at the end of this road (the majority is now covered by Lake Powell). The present day dirt road runs 62 miles from Escalante and dead-ends at that dam lake. It is the access road to many of the hikes featured in this book, including Peek-A-Boo and Spooky Slot Canyons, Zebra Slot Canyon, Coyote Gulch, and Willow Gulch/40 Mile Gulch. It is worth noting that much of this road is no longer within the former bounds of Grand Staircase-Escalante National

Cedar Wash Arch

Covered Wagon Natural Bridge

Monument (and the last few miles are within Glen Canyon National Recreation Area).

Roadside Attractions

Cedar Wash Arch and Covered Wagon Natural Bridge: Located off Cedar Wash Road, both features require about a 0.5-mile hike.

Devil's Garden: A scenic area of sculpted hoodoos 12 miles from Highway 12.

Dance Hall Rock: Historic Mormon meeting place.

Devil's Garden

Highway 12 and "The Hogback"

The scenic road connects US Route 89 with Utah State Route 24 in Torrey, and provides modern-day access between the

The Hogback

towns of Escalante and Boulder, Utah (previously the only route was via Hell's Backbone Road and the more primitive Boulder Mail Trail before that). This stretch of highway provides access directly to several hikes including Bighorn Canyon, Upper Calf

Creek Falls, Escalante River, and Phipps Wash. The Hogback refers to the stretch of road that traverses a narrow ridge of slickrock in between Boulder and Escalante on Highway 12. The Hogback itself offers exceptional views of the surrounding canyons and straddles the drainages of Calf Creek and Boulder Creek. Both the Burr Trail and the northern end of Cottonwood Canyon are accessed via Highway 12.

Roadside Attractions

100 Hand Panel: Rock art panel accessed via the Escalante Bridge trailhead. Requires a short hike.

Boulder Airstrip: Interesting historic landing strip for access to Boulder, located near Boulder Mail trailhead.

The Burr Trail

The Burr Trails spans 67.4 miles from Boulder to Lake Powell's Bullfrog Marina, passing through Grand Staircase-Escalante National Monument, Capitol Reef National Park, and Glen Canyon National Recreation Area. The first 28 miles near Boulder are paved, and in 2019 a new section was controversially chip sealed by the BLM near Capitol Reef National Park. Both the BLM and the Southern Utah Wilderness Alliance continue to butt heads about whether the rest of the road should be paved. The mostly dirt road requires 4WD especially toward its end. It is named for John Atlantic Burr, who developed a trail to move cattle between winter and summer pastures. Notable Grand Staircase-Escalante National Monument attractions accessed from and along the road include

The Gulch, Singing Canyon, the Circle Cliffs, the Wolverine Loop, Little Death Hollow, and the Escalante River.

Roadside Attractions

Wolverine Petrified Wood Forest: Walk the unique Wolverine Canyon filled with ancient petrified wood.

Singing Canyon Slot: Easily accessed slot off the road for those with kids or old knees. Known for its acoustics, sing away!

Highway 89

This staple southwest route is used within Grand Staircase-Escalante to primarily commute to hikes between Page, Arizona, and Kanab, Utah. The Wahweap Hoodoos, The Toadstools, Buckskin Gulch, The Nautilus, Johnson Canyon Road, and the southern reach of Cottonwood Canyon Road are all off Highway 89. Highway 89 is also used as the primary route from the south to reach the northern outposts of the monument (Escalante and Boulder) via Highway 12.

The Nautilus

Paria Movie Set

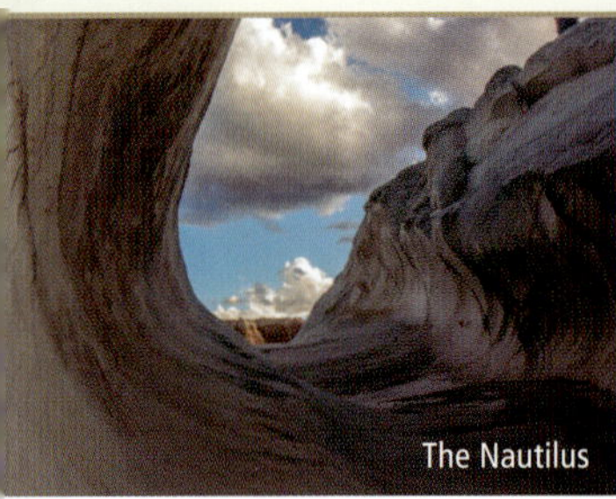

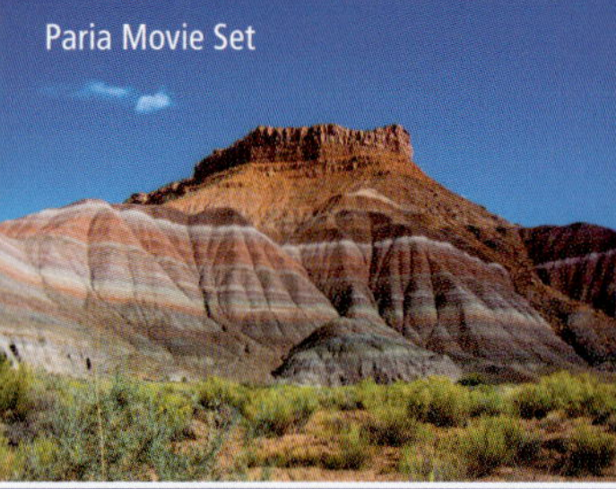

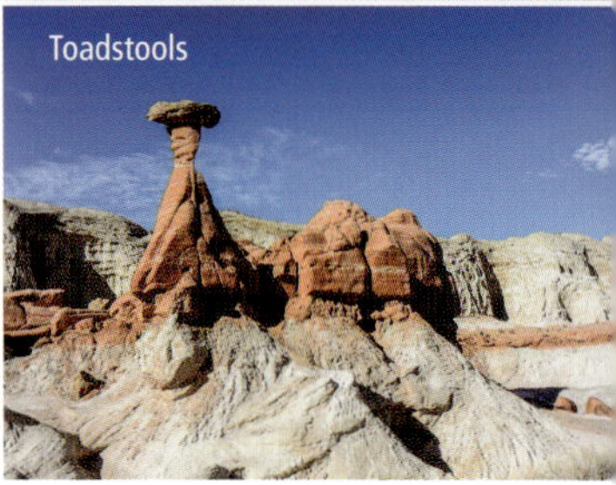
Toadstools

Roadside Attractions

The Nautilus: Interesting wave-like feature located off White House Road.

The Toadstools: Interesting hoodoos about a 15-minute hike from your car.

Paria Movie Set and Old Townsite: Site of an old movie set (since arsoned) and an old Mormon settlement.

Mollies Nipple: Anomalous peak guarding over the Grand Staircase, 4WD can get you to the base, and a difficult scramble can put you up top.

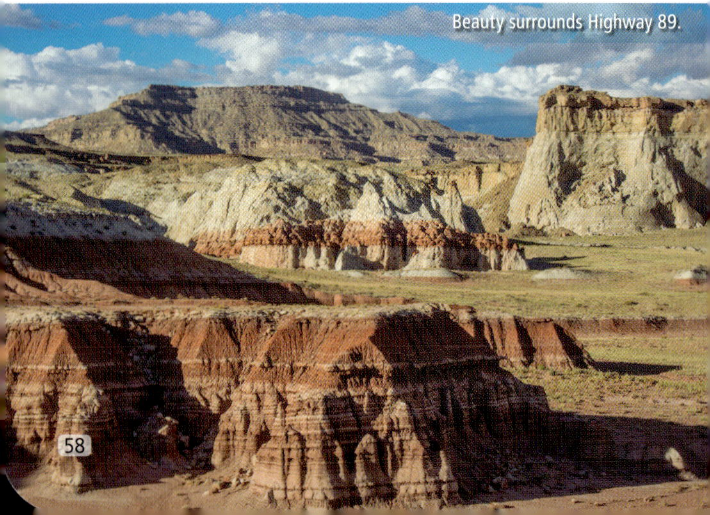
Beauty surrounds Highway 89.

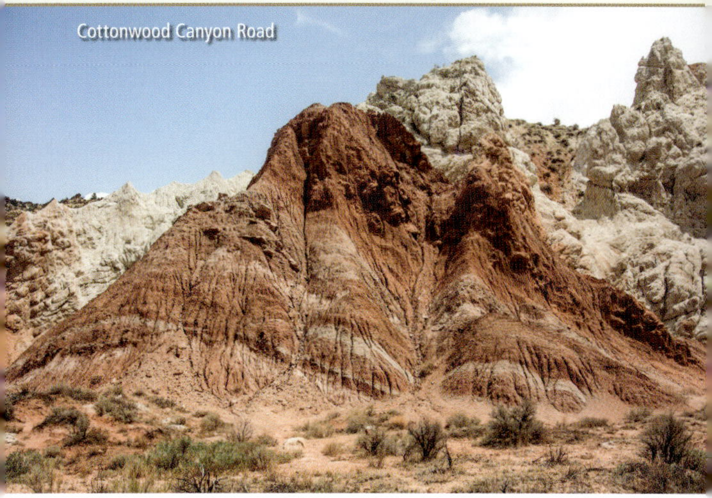

Cottonwood Canyon Road

Cat Stair Canyon Petroglyphs/Car Wash: Highway 89 cuts through The Cockscomb at this canyon. See if you can find the petroglyphs and the erosion-control methods that offer up this wash's name.

Cottonwood Canyon Road

For 46 miles Cottonwood Canyon Road bisects the southern portion of the monument and parallels The Cockscomb. It offers access to the zone's spectacular hiking (Yellow Rock, Cottonwood Narrows, Lower Hackberry) and connects Highway 89 between Big Water and Kanab with Highway 12 and Cannonville to the north.

Roadside Attractions

Grosvenor Arch: A main attraction named to honor a president of the National Geographic Society. An easy stroll to an impressive double arch.

Grosvenor Arch

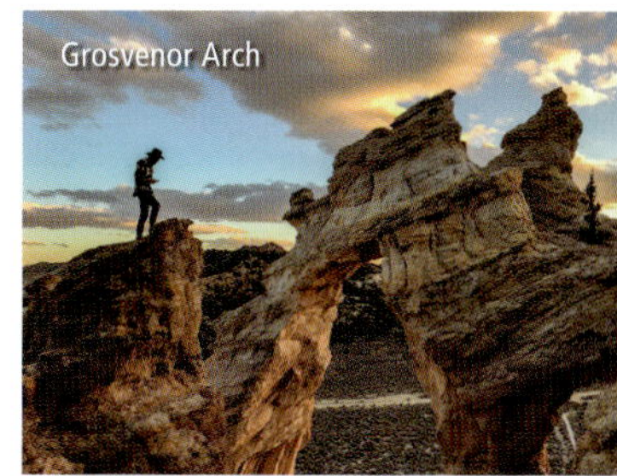

The Paria Box: Where the Paria River cuts its way through The Cockscomb.

The Cockscomb: A geological oddity running north to south along Cottonwood Creek.

Skutumpah Road

Skutumpah Road is 34 miles long within the boundaries of Grand Staircase-Escalante National Monument and runs from Glendale to Cannonville. It can be accessed just outside Kanab via Johnson Canyon Road. Several notable hikes are accessed from this road (including Lick Wash and Bull Valley Gorge), which passes over the infamous Bull Valley Gorge Bridge, where a truck remains wedged in the slot canyon below. The drive itself is beautiful and offers excellent views of the pink, gray, and white cliffs of the Grand Staircase.

Roadside Attractions

Bull Valley Gorge's Stuck Truck: If the hike through Bull Valley Gorge fringes your nerves, walk to the edge and view the infamous stuck truck.

Paunsaugunt Plateau: Bordering to the north, the expansive plateau and its cliff breaks offer scenic views, including those of Bryce Canyon.

Hell's Backbone

Hell's Backbone was constructed in 1933 by the Civilian Conservation Corps (CCC) to connect the town of Boulder (one of the last frontier towns that still received mail by mule—"Boulder Mail Trail") with Escalante. It was originally named "Poison Road" for the certain death facing anyone who drove off the often 800-foot drops straddling this road. This 35-mile stretch of dirt road climbs up to 9,000 feet, traverses the narrow spine of Hell's Backbone via a dramatic 109-foot bridge, and passes through Sand Creek and the Box Death Hollow Wilderness.

Roadside Attractions

Hell's Backbone Bridge: Heart-stopping drops to either side, overlooking the Box Death Hollow Wilderness.

Johnson Canyon Road

Starting just outside the town of Kanab (11 miles due east), Johnson Canyon Road remains paved for its 18 miles and is the primary access point for Skutumpah Road and Lick Wash, Bull Valley Gorge and Willis Creek. The vermillion, white, gray, and pink cliffs of the Grand Staircase are all visible on this drive.

Smoky Mountain
Road

Smoky Mountain Road

Running 78 miles from Escalante (Scenic Byway 12) to the shores of Lake Powell near the town of Big Water (US Highway. 89), Smoky Mountain Road is the main human access point to and across the Kaiparowits Plateau. Four-wheel-drive with high clearance is suggested for this route. The southernmost stretch is not for timid drivers (white knuckle warning for passengers as well). The road drops 1,200 feet toward Lake Powell via the precipitous Kelly Grade, a treacherous stretch of one-lane winding road flanked by sheer drop-offs. The road is named for local legend Don Kelly, who graded and built the road himself because no one else had the courage to do so. While no hikes in this guidebook take off from Smoky Mountain Road, driving its length is a great way to get a taste of the Kaiparowits Plateau and surrounding area.

Roadside Attractions

Kelly Grade: Perilous road section descending the Kaiparowits, which makes the much more popular Moki Dugway in Bears Ears look like a stroll.

Burning Hills Lookout: Look down into one of the last truly wild places in the Lower 48, the Burning Hills.

House Rock Valley Road

Connecting Highway 89A north of Marble Canyon in Arizona to the Kaibab Plateau above the Vermillion Cliffs, House Rock

Valley Road serves as the jumping-off point to such classic hikes as The Wave, the Arizona Trail, and Buckskin Gulch. This 30-mile dirt road is so named after the white and turquoise feature located on the north side of 89A. The southern end offers a unique opportunity to view nesting California condors. These critically endangered modern dinosaurs soar high above the cliffs with wingspans known to reach up to ten feet!

Roadside Attractions

White Pocket: Kanab advertises this as "The Wave without the lottery."

The Wave: The oh-so-infamous Wave exploded in popularity after it was featured in an operating system's stock photo selection. A lottery has been in place ever since, allowing only a few visitors a day.

Coyote Buttes: While permits are required via the lottery for North and now South Coyote Buttes, it's still worth a try in this otherworldly section of The Cockscomb.

Arizona Trail: The 830-mile-long AZT starts/ends at the trailhead just to the west of the road at the Stateline Trailhead and Campground.

Condor Viewing Area: Located on the southern end of House Rock Valley Road, pull over here and you may get lucky with a condor sighting.

Thru-Hiking

Thru-hiking options abound. The following are relatively popular established routes in the area:

The Escalante River, the Bridge to Lake Powell: Ninety or so miles of meandering, deep red wall canyon riparian bliss. Simply start at the bridge and hike down till you hit the lake. Hell, fill up that air mattress and keep floating.

Wire Pass and the Paria River to Lee's Ferry: One of the most popular backpacking routes in the Southwest, 42 miles of slot canyon and narrows will eventually get you to the Colorado River at Lee's Ferry in Marble Canyon.

Hayduke Trail: We don't know if Hayduke lives or not, what we do know is that the Hayduke Trail is quickly becoming a classic route for thru-hikers looking for something a bit more challenging than the manicured maintained trails of other scenic thru-hikes. This 800+ mile route hits all five of Utah's National Parks, and even traverses across, you guessed it, the Grand Staircase.

Arizona Trail: This 830-mile route from the Utah border to Mexico traverses some of wildest places Arizona has to offer. Although not technically in the monument, this trail start/ends off the nearby House Rock Valley Road.

Great Western Trail: This nearly 4,500-mile route, which includes sections of both motorized and non-motorized use, runs from Canada all the way deep into Mexico. The section that crosses the monument parallels Johnson Canyon Road from north to south and is motorized, although painfully sandy and remote.

Notable Mentions

This guidebook is nowhere near comprehensive. The deeper you dive into this place, the more you will realize that you have barely scratched the surface. If the 25 included routes don't satisfy your itch, here is a list of notable entries that didn't make the cut.

1. **Lower Hackberry Canyon/Stone Donkey/Sam Pollock Arch**: Access to Upper Hackberry Creek is via Round Valley Draw (see hike 18). The lower section eventually ends with its confluence with Cottonwood Creek near the start of the Yellow Rock hike (see hike 19).

2. **Harris Wash/Silver Creek Falls**: This popular side canyon of the Escalante offers great backpacking and multi-day

jaunts when combined with the Escalante and/or the many hikes in this book that start and/or end at Harris Wash.

3. **Twentyfive Mile Canyon**: Another popular side canyon of the Escalante. Great for river access or multi-day backpacking trips.

4. **Scorpion Gulch**: Hard to get to, this side drainage of the Escalante offers solitude in a remarkable place. Usually only accessed as a side trip of longer backpacking trips along the Escalante.

5. **Pine Creek Box Trail**: Technically not a part of the monument, the Box Death Hollow Wilderness borders GSENM to the northwest just outside of the town of Escalante. This popular hike follows a beautiful canyon, traversing many life zones as you climb or descend from the higher plateaus above to the lower desert and Navajo Sandstone.

6. **Upper Gulch**: The northern upper section of The Gulch is often utilized as access to the scenic Laminate Arch.

7. **Sidestep Canyon/White Rock Hoodoo Loop**: This side canyon of Wahweap Creek is absolutely worthy of exploring. The upper section is where the goods are. It can be combined with the White Rock Hoodoo Loop farther to the west.

8. **Edmaier's Secret**: Usually accessed via Wire Pass, this hard-to-locate area of geological oddities is worth the endless days stumbling around the dry desert it will take to find it—unless you cheat and look it up.

9. **Davis Gulch**: Davis Gulch is a possible if not likely spot of the infamous Everett Ruess' disappearance in 1934.

10. **Sunset Arch**: A couple miles east of the Water Tank trailhead on 40 Mile Ridge Road stands a series of arches, the first and most popular being Sunset Arch. See how many others you can find.

"It is a lovely and terrible wilderness, harshly and beautifully colored, broken and worn until its bones are exposed, its great sky without a smudge of taint from Technocracy, and in hidden corners and pockets under its cliffs the sudden poetry of springs. Save a piece of country like that intact, and it does not matter in the slightest that only a few people every year will go into it. That is precisely its value. Roads would be a desecration, crowds would ruin it. But those who haven't the strength or youth to go into it and live can simply sit and look. And if they can't even get to the places on the Aquarius Plateau where the present roads will carry them, they can simply contemplate the idea, take pleasure in the fact that such a timeless and uncontrolled part of earth is still there. These are some of the things wilderness can do for us. That is the reason we need to put into effect, for its preservation, some other principle that the principles of exploitation or "usefulness" or even recreation. We simply need that wild country available to us, even if we never do more than drive to its edge and look in. For it can be a means of reassuring ourselves of our sanity as creatures, a part of the geography of hope."

—Wallace Stegner

1. Peek-A-Boo Slot and Spooky Gulch (Dry Creek)

DISTRICT:	Canyons of the Escalante/Hole-In-The-Rock Road
RATING:	Easy to Moderate
DISTANCE:	3–5 miles (depending on options)
ELEVATION GAIN:	+/–500 feet
ROUND-TRIP TIME:	2–4 hours
MAP:	Trails Illustrated #710, Canyons of the Escalante
NEAREST LANDMARK:	Escalante River

COMMENT: A trip to the narrow tributaries of the Dry Fork of Coyote Gulch is not just a hike—it's a chance to play! Climb over pour-overs, squeeze through tight narrows, and crawl through the intricate waterholes of these slots that can be connected as a loop or enjoyed in separate shorter outings.

Peek-A-Boo is named for a series of interlinked standing holes in the rock and involves scrambling up a series of Moki steps over a stagnant pool of cool water. Most will have to get on their hands and knees at some point. Reaching the dark Navajo cross-bedded rock walls of Spooky Gulch via Peek-A-Boo requires basic route finding. While ropes and gear are not required, some technical scrambling, rock hopping, and potential cold water crossings will be necessary to complete these hikes.

If you are hesitant about the scramble up to Peek-A-Boo Slot or at all concerned with claustrophobia, take a warm-up hike through Dry Creek, which is the most open-area slot, completely non-technical, and requires only walking.

For the adventurous spirits on the other end of the spectrum, Brimstone Canyon is a worthwhile addition to a day spent in the Dry Fork of Coyote Gulch. Brimstone is extremely narrow and notoriously filled with deep cold water (bring a wetsuit if you are serious about exploring this one).

GETTING THERE: From Escalante, drive east on Highway 12 for 5.0 miles. Turn right onto Hole-In-The-Rock Road. Continue for 26

Peek into the underworld of the desert.

miles and make a left at the Dry Fork junction (BLM 252). After about 0.75 mile, stay left at the fork and continue to the trailhead. The last 0.5 mile or so has some sections (especially during weather) that can make the unseasoned question not getting that rental insurance in St. George. If so, pull anywhere off the road and hike the remainder to the trailhead. **See "A Note on Roads in GSENM,"** page 54.

THE ROUTE: From your car, follow the cairns down to the bottom of Dry Fork for 0.5 mile. Going upcanyon takes you into an unnamed narrow of Dry Creek that immediately slots up (4 to 8-foot canyon) for 1.0 mile and is an excellent choice for kids and people who don't like scrambling. You can turn around here to head back to the wash or climb up and out and follow the rim trail back to your starting point, or toward Peek-A-Boo.

Moki your way up into the slot.

Playing slots.

From Dry Creek, Peek-A-Boo is about 100 yards downcanyon. Note the seasonal pool of water at the entrance and Moki steps required to climb to enter the slot. The canyon itself is about 1.0 mile, crossing multiple seasonal pools of water and presenting hikers with intermittent scrambling. From the top of Peek-A-Boo you can follow a faint rim trail and cairns for about 0.5 mile to the top of Spooky Gulch. Descend down into Spooky, which requires a somewhat steep drop at one point (ropes aren't necessary—if you are not capable of descending without one this hike is not for you). For all routes, exit back out to Dry Fork.

For those interested in avoiding scrambling and climbing, and yet still experience some of the magic of these slot canyons, it is possible to enter Peek-A-Boo from the top and turn around at first difficulty. This is also possible in Spooky Gulch—enter from the bottom and turn around at first difficulty.

To access Brimstone Canyon (if you dare), continue downcanyon past the exit of Spooky Gulch until a major canyon joins on the left. This is Brimstone. Head upcanyon for a while until it narrows and you are inevitably turned around.

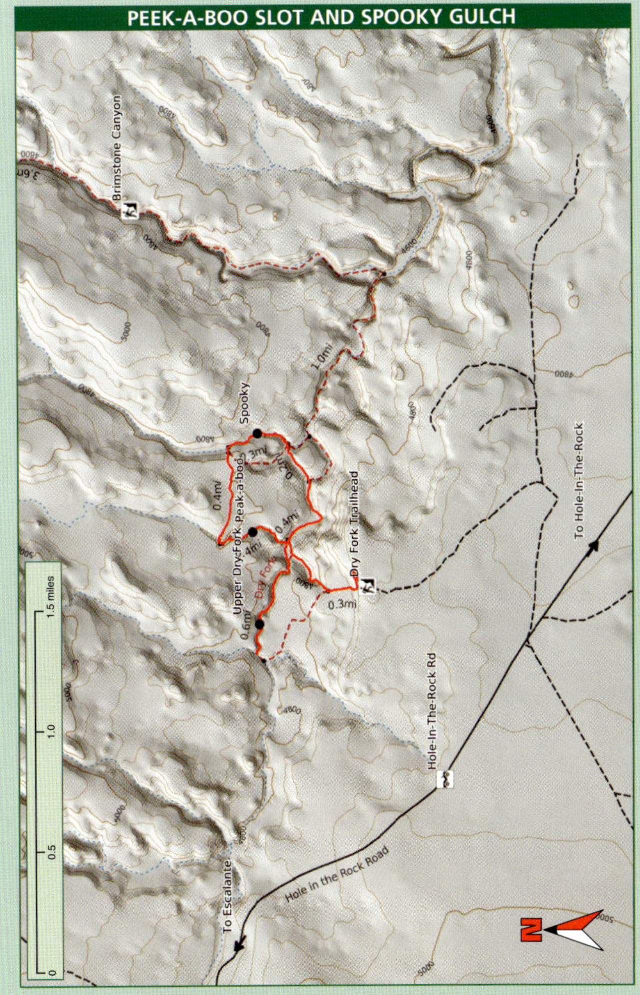
Brimstone Canyon
3.6mi
Spooky
Peek-a-boo
Upper Dry Fork
Dry Fork
Dry Fork Trailhead
0.3mi
0.4mi
0.4mi
0.4mi
0.4mi
0.6mi
0.3mi
0.2mi
1.0mi
4800
4800
4800
5000
5000
5000
5000
To Hole-In-The-Rock
Hole-In-The-Rock Rd
Hole in the Rock Road
To Escalante
1.5 miles
1.0
0.5
0
N

2. Hurricane Wash to Coyote Gulch

DISTRICT:	Canyons of the Escalante/Hole-In-The-Rock Road
RATING:	Moderate
DISTANCE:	26 miles round trip
ELEVATION GAIN:	+/– 900 feet
ROUND-TRIP TIME:	2–3 days
MAP:	Trails Illustrated #710, Canyons of the Escalante
NEAREST LANDMARK:	Escalante River

COMMENT: Anyone who hikes through the hot, dusty, and exposed miles of Hurricane Wash will be rewarded with numerous arches, waterfalls, tinajas, and eventually the Escalante River, in the lair of Coyote Gulch. While Coyote Gulch technically lies within the boundaries of Glen Canyon National Recreation Area, access to this gem requires starting at and hiking through the bounds of Grand Staircase-Escalante National Monument—it's worth blurring the lines.

While water is abundant in the canyon via natural springs, falls, and the river, always come prepared with your own stash and, of course, bring a filtration system. Expect water conditions to fluctuate dramatically throughout the year. While this route can be done at any time of the year, those who enjoy swimming will appreciate the experience of this canyon to its fullest during warm weather (late spring to early fall).

Coyote Gulch is a popular hiking destination, so if you are craving total solitude let that vision go, but do this route anyway—the other people are all here for a clear reason.

Wild spring water.

Always camp in established sites, pack it in and out, and for the love of wild places please leave no trace. Human waste bags are required on this hike and are available for a fee at the Escalante BLM visitors center.

GETTING THERE: From Escalante, head east on Highway 12 for 5.0 miles. Turn right on Hole-In-The-Rock Road. Continue for 34 miles and park at the signed trailhead for Hurricane Wash.

THE ROUTE: From the trailhead, follow the sandy single-track trail along Hurricane Wash for several miles. This section is slow moving and the least interesting of the entire route— stay the course. Wide-set walls of red sandstone will begin to rise, vegetation will increase, and water will start to seep as you near the junction with Coyote Gulch (~5.0 miles).

Once in Coyote Gulch you will encounter running streams, dripping springs, pools of water, and waterfalls running at fluctuating levels. Water sources are plentiful but all will require filtration unless you are knowledgeable in sourcing spring water.

Legendary Lobo Arch.

Stephen's Arch rising above the Escalante.

Lobo Arch (also referred to as Jacob Hamblin Arch) just about marks your halfway point down to the Escalante River. There are plentiful campsites and water sources between Lobo and Coyote Natural Bridge (just under 2.0 miles downcanyon), making this zone an ideal stopping point for overnight trips.

The following sections of the route feature several waterfalls, pools, and pour-overs that can be navigated simply by looking for well-defined sections of single-track marking the route.

More water will be present along the route as you near the confluence with the Escalante River. We recommend exploring and following the Escalante both up and down stream before turning around and heading back along the same route to your vehicle.

A very popular alternative route is the loop route out of Water Tank Trailhead/40 Mile Ridge Trailhead, accessed via 40 Mile Ridge Road (see map). This route descends the canyon walls either at the Jacob Hamblin Arch, or the impressive Crack-In-The-Wall. These trailheads, *especially* 40 Mile Ridge trailhead, require 4WD. The deep sand is no joke.

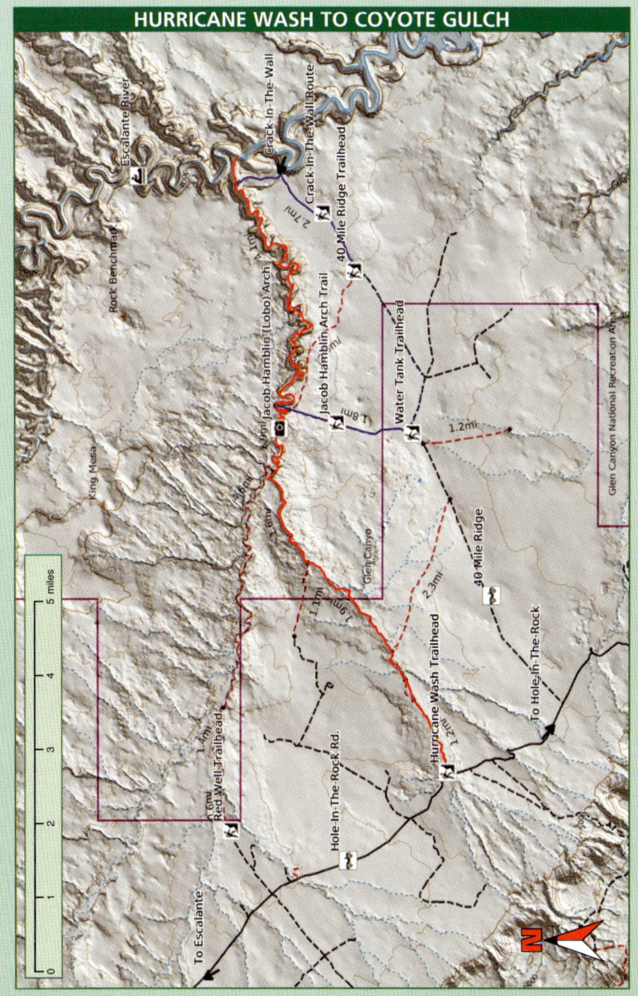
Escalante River
Crack-In-The-Wall
Crack-In-The-Wall Route
Crack-In-The-Wall Trailhead
40 Mile Ridge Trailhead
2.7mi
Rock Benchmark
Jacob Hamblin (Lobo) Arch
1.1mi
Jacob Hamblin Arch Trail
Water Tank Trailhead
1.8mi
Glen Canyon National Recreation Area
1.2mi
King Mesa
1.6mi
Glen Canyo
40 Mile Ridge
2.3mi
1.1mi
1.9mi
Hurricane Wash Trailhead
To Hole-In-The-Rock
Red Well Trailhead
1.4mi
1.6mi
Hole-In-The-Rock Rd.
1.2mi
To Escalante
5 miles
0   1   2   3   4   5
N

3. Egypt 3

DISTRICT:	Canyons of the Escalante/Hole-In-The-Rock Rd.
RATING:	Difficult
DISTANCE:	8 miles
ELEVATION GAIN:	1,300 feet
ROUND-TRIP TIME:	3–8 hours
MAP:	Trails Illustrated #710, Canyons of the Escalante
NEAREST LANDMARK:	Escalante River

COMMENT: With minimal obstacles found only at the beginning of this canyon, Egypt 3 is one of the longest continually walkable slot canyons. This is especially noteworthy as the other Egypt slot canyons are some of the most technically difficult and dangerous (Class 4 and 5). Passing through the ribbon of narrow walls, less than a foot apart at their tightest quarter, without pause feels dizzying. The end of the route described here features a few mini arches and peek holes before the final dryfall and pool. The exit route along the

The Cursed Temple of Ishtar.

rim provides a radically different perspective, a bird's-eye view of the slot canyon and sweeping views of the Hole-In-The-Rock region across rolling colorful slickrock expanses.

GETTING THERE: From Escalante, head east on Highway 12 for 5.0 miles. Turn right on Hole-In-The-Rock Road. Continue for 16 miles and turn left at the signed road for Egypt. Reset your odometer here. At 3.5 miles you will cross 25 Mile Wash. There is a

The Embalmed Dunes of Isis.

pullout for parking here for those looking to start a backpacking route down 25 Mile Wash to the Escalante. There are six Egypt Canyons, (1, 1.5, 2, 3, 4, and 5), numbered west to east, all running relatively north to south off the Egypt Bench/Allen Dump. You will cross the head canyon of the first three canyons before arriving at the parking area for Egypt 3. None of the canyons are signed so pay attention to your odometer. At 8.0 miles you will cross a rough section of slickrock very near the large rappel into Egypt 2. You will know it when you cross it. When your odometer reads 9.0 miles you should reach another wash and you will see a white spire out on the left (to the north) of the road. Find a place to park off the road; this is the start of Egypt 3.

The last few miles of the road are likely impassable to the low-clearance passenger vehicles that descend upon

Narrow contemplation in Egypt.

A Pharaoh's Hallway.

Escalante from St. George rental shops. While potentially accessible by a capable driver via 2WD sedan, for most, high clearance could not be more highly recommended.

THE ROUTE: Save for a few chockstones and deep pools, the most difficult part of this hike is locating the entrance point into the canyon. From the parking area, head south and descend the initial 0.25 mile or so downcanyon. All roads should end at a very large dryfall. If you are looking for big rappel, then continue on down, but for most, this is obviously not your entrance point. Trend left along the eastern rim of the canyon for several hundred yards. Stick close to the rim as you will quickly come upon a side canyon to Egypt 3. Find a way to drop down onto the slickrock expanse, locating the occasional cairn, and continue until you arrive at the floor of Egypt 3. Once in the canyon you will encounter a few tricky areas requiring downclimbing, slick spots to slide down, and a couple deep potholes that can be averted by those tall enough for full body stemming, or simply just wade across the shallow waters.

From here the route is straight and very narrow, broken by a few wider areas and exit opportunities for those not able to make the squeezes. Egypt 3 consists of three sections of narrows all offering something a bit different. The canyon itself is almost 4.0 miles long until it drops into 25 Mile Wash at an impassable dryfall. This marks your turnaround. For those that feel capable, you can return the exact way you came, but for most it won't be possible to climb up what you (probably) slid down to get to this point.

"Sick action shot, bro."

Even those who can return upcanyon, the optional rim route is highly recommended, as it traverses some very impressive country, otherworldly expanses of colorful slickrock and geologic oddities. It passes through "The Embalmed Dunes of Isis," "The Scarab Mounds," and "The Cursed Temple of Ishtar,"—or so the authors informally named these impressive features.

From the turnaround, head upcanyon the way you came until you reach the large open area and an easy climb to your right (east). Gain the bench above and continue heading north, keeping Egypt 3 far below you and on your left. Navigate the unearthly terrain as you head north, and don't worry if Egypt 3 goes out of sight for a while. Just keep heading north, gaining the final bench on top of the Egypt Plateau. Head northwest back to your vehicle and if you aren't sure where you are at, just head north until you hit the road, then head west to where you parked.

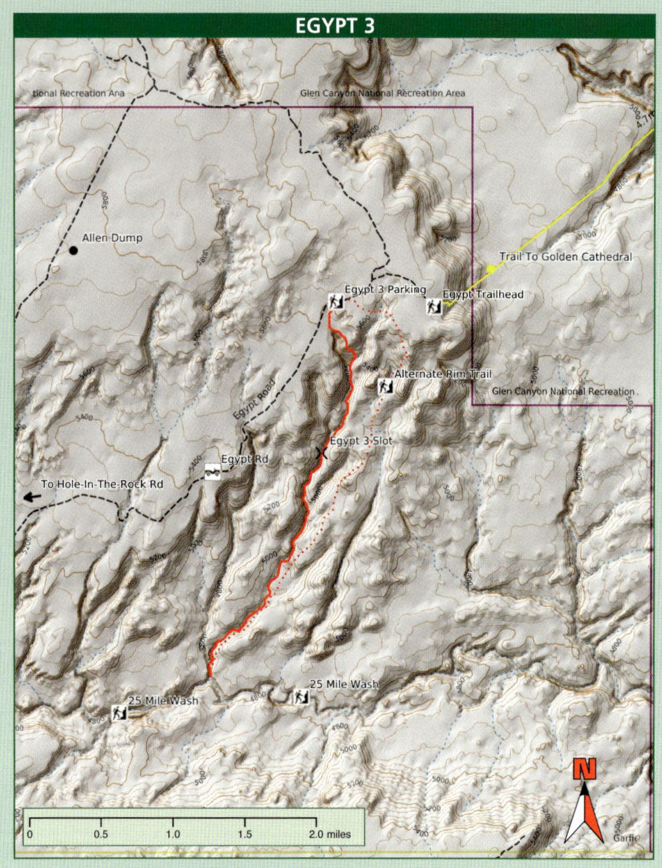
tional Recreation Ana
Glen Canyon National Recreation Area
Allen Dump
Trail To Golden Cathedral
Egypt 3 Parking
Egypt Trailhead
Alternate Rim Trail
Glen Canyon National Recreation
Egypt Road
Egypt 3 Slot
Egypt Rd
To Hole-In-The-Rock Rd
25 Mile Wash
25 Mile Wash
25 Mile Wash
0
0.5
1.0
1.5
2.0 miles
N
Garfi

4. Neon Canyon and the Golden Cathedral

DISTRICT:	Canyons of the Escalante
RATING:	Moderate
DISTANCE:	9 miles
ELEVATION GAIN:	1,500 feet
ROUND-TRIP TIME:	4–8 hours
MAP:	Trails Illustrated #710, Canyons of the Escalante
NEAREST LANDMARK:	Escalante River

COMMENT: Follow the Neon Canyon delights to the Golden Cathedral, where you can wash away your sinful cravings for a full-strength beer (you are in Utah after all) in the gleaming waters beneath the skylight openings. Tucked within a world of sandstone, this is the closest you're going to get to a dive bar, anyway. We suggest you bring your own cold one (and a picnic) to bask in the light from above you before you retrace your steps through Neon Canyon, across the Escalante River, and up the very steep and exposed slickrock to the

Follow the Neon Canyon lights to the holy Golden Cathedral.

A golden baptism. Glory hallelujah!

trailhead. This is one of the area's most popular hikes, so expect to cross paths with other seekers on your pilgrimage. Be aware of poison ivy on this hike.

GETTING THERE: From Escalante, head east on Highway 12 for 5.0 miles. Turn right on Hole-In-The-Rock Road. Continue for 16 miles and turn left at the signed road for Egypt. After 9.5 sandy, washed-out, fender-scraping miles, turn right at the sign creatively labeled "trailhead" and go a bit farther until arrival at the aforementioned "trailhead."

The last few miles of Egypt Road are likely impassable to the low-clearance passenger vehicles that descend upon Escalante from St. George rental shops. While potentially accessible by a capable driver via 2WD sedan, for most, high clearance could not be more highly recommended.

THE ROUTE: From your car, head directly east toward the Escalante River, locate the most conspicuous footpath you can, and drop off the bench down a series of steep and well-cairned slickrock slopes and down into the desert. The entire route up until the Escalante is extremely well-cairned and you should be able to stay on route with relative ease. The trail continues on a bench between the two upper canyons of Fence Canyon, eventually dropping off to hiker's right via

Come ye seekers, bow down and worship the wilderness.

a few switchbacks and down to the canyon floor. Continue down Fence Canyon until you arrive at the Escalante. Go swimming, then wade on downcanyon for about 1.0 mile. Stay on the left side of the canyon and keep an eye out for Neon Canyon, which is the first side canyon coming in from the left. Find the trail and continue up Neon Canyon, avoiding the poison ivy, until it dead-ends at the Golden Cathedral and those tantalizing neon lights. Once you get your fix, head back to the Escalante the way you came, and back to your car.

Technical canyoneers can continue down the Escalante to the next canyon on the left and explore the Ringtail Slot. Hikers may wish to add on a trek to lower Choprock Canyon. Backpackers and packrafters can continue down or up the Escalante, as the Egypt trailhead is a great put in/exit point for multi-day adventures.

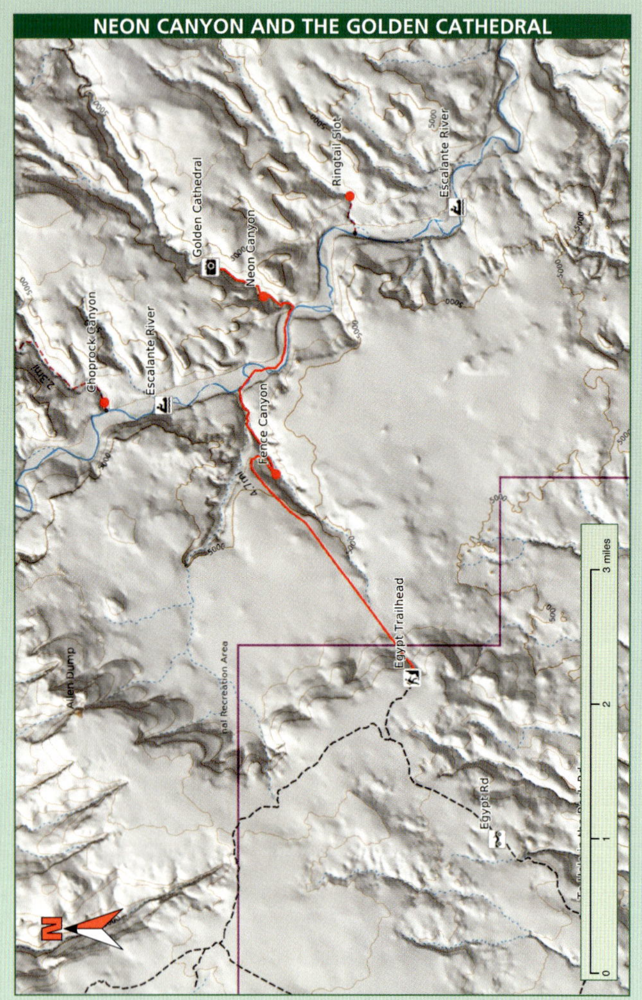
Ringtail Slot
Escalante River
Golden Cathedral
Neon Canyon
Choprock Canyon
Escalante River
2.3 mi.
Fence Canyon
4.7 mi.
Allen Dump
nal Recreation Area
Egypt Trailhead
Egypt Rd.
3 miles
2
1
0
N

5. Willow Wash and 40 Mile Gulch

DISTRICT:	Canyons of the Escalante/Hole-In-The-Rock Road
RATING:	Difficult
DISTANCE:	9–13 miles
ELEVATION GAIN:	500 feet
ROUND-TRIP TIME:	1–2 Days
MAP:	Trails Illustrated #710, Canyons of the Escalante
NEAREST LANDMARK:	Lake Powell

COMMENT: This loop is a roundtable smorgasbord of the beautiful and unique natural features that the canyons of the Escalante region has to offer—slot canyons, streams, and Broken Bow Arch. While the entirety of this loop falls within the boundaries of the Glen Canyon National Recreation Area, it is a prime example of how the boundaries and jurisdictions are not true landscape distinctions. It is worthwhile to continue downstream from the confluence of 40 Mile Gulch and Willow Wash (at this point a canyon with towering sandstone walls) to the point where Lake Powell's stagnant waters pool up. This point can vary dramatically based on the water levels of the lake and likewise alter the added distance.

40 Mile Gulch includes many sections of water-filled narrows that require swimming at times and climbing waterfalls. The difficulty will increase if you are carrying a heavy or large pack. If you are at all uncomfortable with this sort of terrain, consider an out-and-back of Willow Wash and lower 40 Mile Gulch.

Poison ivy is present in the lower reaches of 40 Mile Gulch. Although avoidable, care should be taken.

GETTING THERE: From Escalante, head east on Highway 12 for 5.0 miles. Turn right on Hole-In-The-Rock Road. Continue for 42 miles passing through the scenic Sooner Rocks and hang a left on Road 276. Go for about 1.5 miles until the obvious trailhead.

THE ROUTE: The route described here is a loop route, and therefore can obviously be done in either direction. It is described and recommended here to start down Willow Wash and out 40 Mile Gulch. The section between 40 Mile Gulch and the Willow Trailhead requires hiking cross country, so navigational skills are required. There are also multiple entry/exit points along Hole-In-The-Rock Road. A car shuttle is possible and options for dropping a vehicle include the Willow Trailhead, Sooner Wash, Carcass Wash, 40 Mile Springs, and others.

Willow Wash is a very popular entry/exit point for packrafting adventures as well. If the Escalante happens to be high enough, floating from Coyote Gulch to Willow Wash makes for a great adventure. Downcanyon via Lake Powell, 50 Mile Creek, Davis Gulch, and a plethora of other canyons offer great packrafting excursions.

From the Willow Trailhead, head down the sand dune toward the obvious canyon in front of you. Keep an eye out

Waterfalls and swimming holes—a brave hiker's reward.

for the sombrero-looking rock formation just outside the trailhead. Make sure you trend right of this formation to access the canyon floor. The footpaths leading left will cliff you out, and you will have to backtrack. Once on the canyon floor, continue downcanyon, navigating small narrows, exploring caves, and eventually meeting with Willow Creek proper and the arrival of springs and pools. Once the water starts, be prepared to be wet the rest of the day. After a couple of miles

Walk the wild waterways.

you will arrive at the impressive Broken Bow Arch. Another 0.5 mile or so downcanyon from the arch, the walls will close in, creating a pleasantly cool grotto-esque scene where you will arrive at the confluence of Willow and 40 Mile Gulch/ Creek. Take a left joining with 40 Mile Gulch, or (recommended) continue down Willow Creek toward Lake Powell. The trail downcanyon from here can be hard to follow and requires bushwhacking at times, but hikers that brave the trek will be rewarded with waterfalls, swimming, interesting rock formations, and arrival at the great evaporation and silt tank known as Lake Powell.

From the lake, retrace your steps and hike upstream to the 40 Mile Gulch confluence. Take 40 Mile Gulch and head upcanyon, wading the many pools of 40 Mile Creek. Poison ivy is present but avoidable in these lower sections, so be alert. After a ways, the canyon narrows, forcing the creek

A look through the Broken Bow.

Sooner: Just another long dusty wash.

through tight passageways and deep pools, often cascading over boulder jams that you must climb. Nothing here is very technical or difficult, but could prove impassable for many depending on skill level and physical ability. Once past the narrows, continue upcanyon and past a large waterfall that is bypassed on the left. Beyond the falls the canyon starts to break up into the head canyons of 40 Mile Gulch, Sooner Wash, Carcass Wash, and a number of other smaller drainages. Trend left for the next few miles, unless you feel like exploring some of these side drainages, which all offer interesting features.

Around 6.0 miles from the Willow Trailhead (excluding the out and back down to the big pond), stay left, and find your way up sandy slopes and slickrock ledges that allow you to gain the top of Sooner Bench. From here it's a cross-country trek back to your car, which you wisely marked with your GPS or applicable phone app, and find your way back to your vehicle. Other options include continuing up Sooner Wash and back to the road, which includes stemming and chimneying up a short slot to escape, or out Carcass Wash.

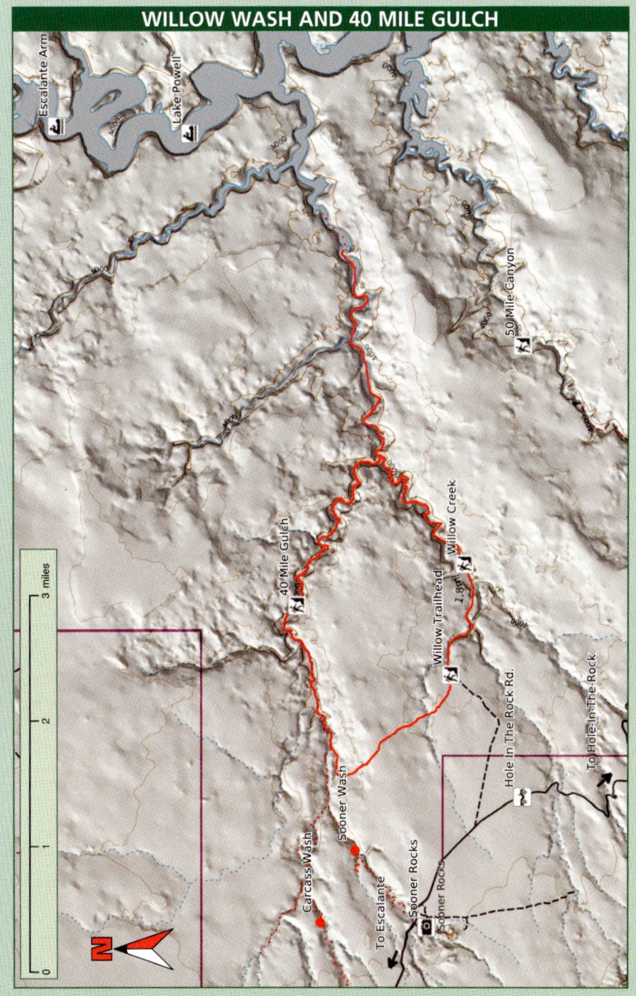

Escalante Arm
Lake Powell
50 Mile Canyon
Willow Creek
40 Mile Gulch
Willow Trailhead
1.8mi
To Hole In The Rock
Hole In The Rock Rd.
Sooner Wash
Carcass Wash
Sooner Rocks
Sooner Rocks
To Escalante
3 miles
2
1
0
N

6. Zebra and Tunnel Slot Canyons

DISTRICT:	Canyons of the Escalante/Hole-In-The-Rock Road
RATING:	Easy
DISTANCE:	5.3 miles for Zebra only; 7 miles with Tunnel
ELEVATION GAIN:	200 feet
ROUND-TRIP TIME:	2–3 hours
MAPS:	Trails Illustrated #710, Canyons of the Escalante
NEAREST LANDMARK:	Hole-In-The-Rock Road

COMMENT: One of the most photographed and name-dropped slot canyons in the area, Zebra Canyon has the crowds to prove it. If solitude is your thing, this is not the place for you, but its relative ease and short distance still make this a hike very much worth taking.

Zebra Canyon itself is short, narrow, and lined in colorful pink and white striped walls. It is not uncommon for this canyon to be filled with water (sometimes waist deep or higher). It is possible to scramble up and out of the canyon to its true end, but it's not necessary to get the full experience of this underground treasure.

The far less visited Tunnel Slot is a unique slot that appears to close up at the top, offering its namesake. Like Zebra, Tunnel is short but still worth the extra walk down the wash.

Note the unique round black rocks scattered among these canyons and the surrounding area. Moqui Marbles are formed when iron oxide encapsulates balls of Navajo Sandstone. Similar rocks have been found on Mars, giving them the nickname "Martian Blueberries." It is illegal to remove them.

Hard not to imagine this slot being made of bacon. Mmmm.

GETTING THERE: From Escalante, head east on Highway 12 for 5.0 miles. Turn right on Hole-In-The-Rock Road. Continue for 8.0 miles and park at the signed trailhead for Zebra Slot Canyon trailhead.

THE ROUTE: The approach to Zebra is on well-defined single track along a sandy wash and sandstone formations. Keep an eye out for cairns, although if you follow the general direction of the wash you will stay on target. At 2.0 miles from the trailhead, the side canyon you have been in will converge with a much larger sandy wash. This is Harris Wash. Trend left, turning up Harris Wash for a 100 yards or so, then cross, leaving Harris Wash and trend right, following the many footpaths toward the side canyon that is Zebra. It will be easy to find. The canyon itself is short, ending for most at the first large pothole a few hundred feet from where the slot starts. The hardy may scramble up a few more turns into the canyon, but the payoff isn't really worth the effort to get a few

A safari through petrified sand dunes to the zoo of Zebra slot canyon.

feet farther. Caution should be exercised when these large potholes are full of water—the inexperienced may not be able to claw their way back out.

Once satisfied with your stripey photos, return to Harris Wash. Or if you desire to continue, turn left and head down-canyon via Harris Wash. In about 1.0 mile you will notice cairns and a footpath leaving the main canyon on your left, and up a side canyon. Turn here and make your way up this drainage, which soon narrows dramatically and forms the aptly named Tunnel Slot. This slot usually has a bit of water in it, but it is wadeable. Once through, you can return the way you came, back to Harris Wash and back to your car, or continue up the drainage that forms Tunnel, which will even-tually top out on a slickrock bench looking over Harris Wash and the surrounding areas. Explore these sweeping seas of slickrock benches and Moqui Marbles while slowly trending westward and back toward the entry wash of Zebra.

Harris Wash
Tunnel Slot
2.8mi
To Spencer Flat Rd
Zebra Slot
0.2mi
0.1mi
0.3mi
Upper Harris Wash
Harris Wash
2.0mi
3.0mi
Trail To Zebra Slot
Zebra and Tunnel Slots Trailhead
To Escalante
Hole in the Rock Road
1.5 miles
1.0
0.5
0

7. Red Breaks and the Cosmic Ashtray

DISTRICT:	Canyons of the Escalante/Hole-In-The-Rock Road
RATING:	Strenuous
DISTANCE:	13 miles
ELEVATION GAIN:	2,500 feet
ROUND-TRIP TIME:	1–2 days
MAP:	Trails Illustrated #710, Canyons of the Escalante
NEAREST LANDMARK:	Escalante River

COMMENT: Take a magical mystery tour of Grand Staircase! Red Breaks is a long, narrow, deep red, and winding slot canyon that will guide you to a cross-country traverse of colorful sandstone ridgelines and valleys with sweeping views of the Escalante canyons. Those who take on the quest (with successful route finding) will be rewarded with a trip to the Cosmic Ashtray—a giant sinkhole in the earth filled with fine orange sand that is wildly more exciting in person than this mundane description, the photos in this book, or even its colorful name can offer.

Now that we have your attention, take note that this is an extremely challenging hike only suited for extremely fit, experienced, and knowledgeable desert hikers. The reasons for the degree of difficulty are numerous: Red Breaks is pencil thin at its narrowest space some larger folks simply will not fit; the obstacles within the canyon require strength (and for most, a team of at least two to help hoist and pull one another up and over boulder and log jams). The cross-country jaunt is completely unmarked, exposed, and over difficult terrain requiring careful route selection. Both Red Breaks

Disclaimer: On this cosmic magical mystery tour rainbows and success not guaranteed.

and the traverse are slow moving, making the distance of this hike deceptive. There are no reliable water sources anywhere on this hike (plan to carry the full supply you will need).

There is an unsettling trend in our current social media–driven culture of well-meaning people attempting hikes far beyond their ability levels in order to get a photo. The Cosmic Ashtray certainly has this appeal and for this reason we hesitated including it in the guidebook. Do yourself a favor and be honest with yourself about your true abilities and fitness on this hike (and all others)—no photo is worth your safety. There are plenty of amazing picturesque attractions that are much easier to get to.

GETTING THERE: From Escalante, head east on Highway 12 for 5.0 miles. Turn right on Hole-In-The-Rock Road. Continue for 10.5 miles and turn left at the signed road for Harris Wash. Stay left at the fork after about 2.5 miles continuing toward Harris Wash, and another 3.5 miles will put you at the signed parking area and trailhead for Harris Wash.

Pumping through
Red Breaks.

Navigation expertise required.

THE ROUTE: From the trailhead, continue down the road for 100 yards or so into Harris Wash. Cross the wash on the jeep road and follow it for a few hundred more yards until you come upon a second dry wash. This is the mouth to a series of canyons collectively referred to as Red Breaks. Head up this wash staying on the canyon floor. You will shortly come upon a split in the canyon where you will want to stay right. After about 3.0 miles the route to the slot canyon leaves the canyon floor you have been in, and climbs the ridge to the left. This trail is usually heavily cairned and easy to locate. This trail puts you above a large dryfall and into a side canyon that contains the notorious slot. If you miss this turn, and you see a large interesting dryfall on your left, you have gone too far and you should turn back and look for the correct route. Once in the side canyon, head up through the narrows battling the many chockstone boulders and extremely narrow and high walls.

For many, some of the scrambling required in Red Breaks will prove to be too difficult. There is no shame in turning back at any point in the slot and returning to your

Take a long smooth drag at the Cosmic Ashtray.

vehicle after an out-and-back hike. For those that do make it through, you can either return the way you came, or attempt to find your way over to the Cosmic Ashtray.

There is no official route to the Ashtray from here. Some people head north and then east to avoid going up and down the head canyons of Red Breaks. Others choose a more direct line going up and down the canyon walls until they get lucky and stumble upon the Ashtray. Either way, this route is only recommended for those comfortable with routefinding and reading topographical features.

If you are lucky enough to find the Ashtray, it is possible to enter into the pothole via a series of modern Moki steps cut into the rock. Descend into the pit, run around, get sand blasted, smoke a cigarette, and make an offering. From the Ashtray, head southwest until you intercept the jeep road that will lead you all the way back to your car.

For those looking to only get your slot on, there is a cross-country route accessed via Spencer Flat Road, which is shorter and only accesses the slot, but that route is not described here.

RED BREAKS AND THE COSMIC ASHTRAY

8. Boulder Mail Trail

DISTRICT:	Canyons of the Escalante/Highway 12
RATING:	Moderate
DISTANCE:	14.5 miles one way (shuttle required)
ELEVATION CHANGE:	2,500 feet gain, 3,500 feet loss (Boulder to Escalante)
ROUND-TRIP TIME:	1–2 days
MAP:	Trails Illustrated #710, Canyons of the Escalante
NEAREST LANDMARK:	Devil's Backbone Road

COMMENTS: The historical Boulder Mail Trail follows the original route traveled by Postal Riders between 1902 and 1940. Remnants of the old telegraph line still pervade the route and can be helpful in navigating some slickrock sections on this cross-country route (don't let the word "trail" fool you). Come prepared with routefinding skills for this traverse of the range between the Boulder Air Strip (and UFO Landing Site) to the Upper Escalante Canyon just outside the town of Escalante. While most choose the Boulder-to-Escalante direction for the hike via a car shuttle, there is nothing wrong with going the opposite direction.

Mail, UFOs, and wild animals send messages along the BMT.

Launch your hike from the Boulder Airport and UFO Landing Site.

Treelines and telephone lines transfer old messages to modern travellers.

This route is exposed, making heat and dehydration serious considerations. Water is available in Sand Creek, Death Hollow, and seasonally at Mamie Creek (2.5, 5.5, and 8.5 miles respectively from the Boulder trailhead). Treating water is always highly advisable.

This hike is often done in combination with Death Hollow and the Upper Escalante Trail (see Hike #9 Death Hollow, page 104). One of the most popular backpacking routes in the area is to start at the Boulder Mail Trail outside of Boulder, down Death Hollow to the upper Escalante, exiting at Highway 12 (see map). Extend your hike with the recommended side-trips to explore both Mamie Creek and its natural bridge, and the rarely visited Sand Creek.

***WARNING:** Poison ivy is unavoidable in the Death Hollow section of this hike. Rinse often in the creek and wear pants and long sleeves if sensitive—or don't go.

GETTING THERE

Boulder Trailhead: From Escalante, head east on Highway 12 toward Boulder. Drive 24 miles over "The Hogback" and turn left on Hell's Backbone Road. The road is heavily signed and easy to locate. After about 100 yards, take your first left down an unmarked dirt road. In 0.25 mile you will cross the Boulder Airstrip and another 0.25 mile will put you at the signed Boulder Mail trailhead.

From Boulder, drive 4.5 miles west toward Escalante on Highway 12, then turn right on Devil's Backbone Road. After about 100 yards, take your first left down an unmarked dirt road. In 0.25 mile you will cross the Boulder Airstrip and another 0.25 mile will put you at the signed Boulder Mail Trailhead.

Escalante Trailhead: On the east side of Escalante, look for the Escalante trailhead signs, and turn north off of Highway 12 toward the cemetery. Stay right and continue down the dirt road for about 0.5 mile before turning left. Another 0.5 mile or so and you will arrive at the trailhead.

THE ROUTE: From the Boulder trailhead, follow the faint single-track path in and out of the piñon/juniper forest, trending southwest. Eventually this will open up to exposed slickrock where you will follow a route marked by cairns. It is advisable to carry a map and compass with you. Don't just blindly follow the cairns—traditional navigational methods will help ensure you remain on course. After about 2.5 miles, you will arrive at the Mail Trail junction with Sand Creek Canyon. This year-round stream is a reliable water source and a great place to cool off. Find your way down toward the water and cross the creek. Locate the faint trail running along the west side of the creek and continue downcanyon for 0.5 mile or so. Just after another dry drainage joins Sand Creek from the north, keep an eye out for cairns leading up slickrock and out of Sand Creek Canyon.

Once you have left Sand Creek, the trail will take you back through the piñon/juniper forests and slickrock, following the old telegraph line. Around 5.0 miles from the trailhead

Hoof it like the historic mailmen of Boulder.

Old gnarled telegraph poles.

you will arrive at a saddle between upper and lower Death Hollow. Veer to the right (north) and follow cairns down into the depths of Death Hollow. Once at the bottom (in the creek), make your way downcanyon (south). After about 0.75 mile, once again the Mail Trail will veer right, up and out of the canyon, regaining the plateau above. Again, this critical junction is nothing more than a few cairns, but is easily found as it is the first non-technical escape route from the canyon, downstream of where you entered.

Once out of Death Hollow, the trail continues southwest, crossing slickrock benches. The route descends into the seasonal Mamie Creek at 8.3 miles (again, a nice side voyage with a natural bridge about 0.75 mile downcanyon). Cross the creek and climb once again toward slickrock benches and piñon/juniper trees. From here the route is very well cairned, perhaps overly so, and remains high until winding down to Pine Creek. Continue along the creek until it joins with the Escalante River, and a bit farther you will arrive at the Escalante trailhead (14.5 miles).

BOULDER MAIL TRAIL

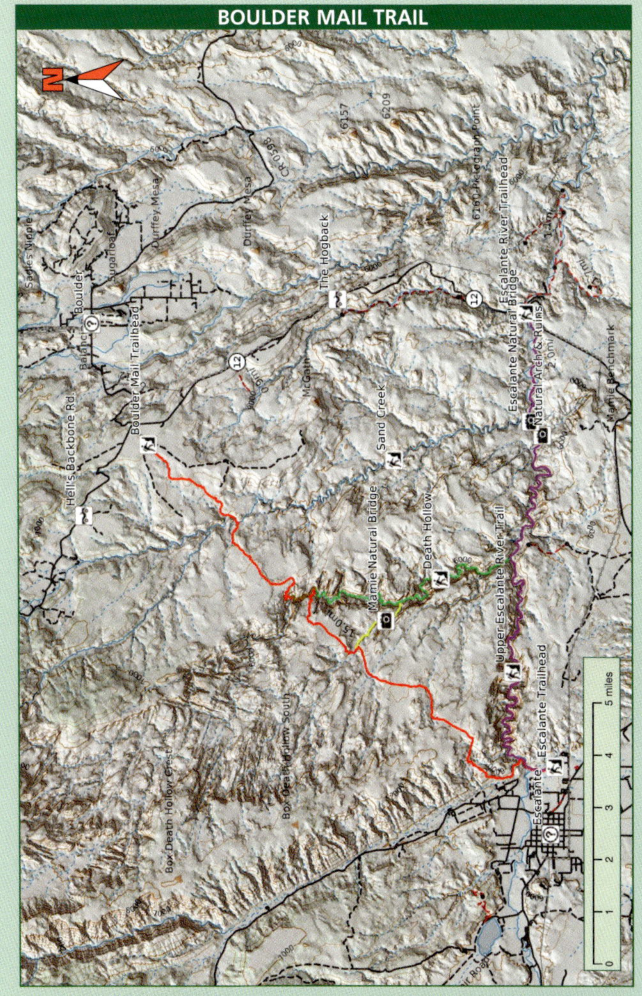

9. Death Hollow

DISTRICT:	Canyons of the Escalante/Highway 12
RATING:	Difficult
DISTANCE:	Approximately 20 miles depending on entry and exit routes
ELEVATION CHANGE:	2,500 feet
ROUND-TRIP TIME:	1–3 days depending on chosen route
MAP:	Trails Illustrated #710, Canyons of the Escalante
NEAREST LANDMARK:	The Hogback

COMMENT: The ominously named Death Hollow is just as likely to intrigue as turn off hikers—a pack animal once fell to its death in the 700-foot drop into this canyon. While this route is certainly nothing to be afraid of, a number of challenges make it best suited for the adventurous, fit, and prepared. There is no marked trailhead to Death Hollow. Entrance and exit points are not easily accessible and require cross-country route finding, making it extremely commit-ting. It requires a car shuttle, unless you want to make this an arduous out and back or even longer loop. Death Hollow constantly crosses in and out of its creek and at times deep pools of water—you will get wet! Both flash floods and hypothermia are a danger if your timing is off (late spring and early fall are best). Perhaps most frightening of all is the nearly constant and unavoidable jungle of poison ivy (leaves of three, let it be) in the canyon. To potentially avoid a rash (no promises), wear long layers, frequently rinse in the creek, and shower with soap and water immediately after this hike.

For those who do take on the challenge, you will witness one of the area's finest canyons, if not only for the beauty of the high sandstone walls contrasted with lush riparian growth,

Don't you want to go into Death Hollow?

but also the exclusivity and effort it requires to experience it. Death Hollow is usually accessed via the Boulder Mail Trail and the Escalante River Trail (for the shuttle, leave a car at each trailhead). This route describes approaching from Boulder via the Boulder Mail Trail, and escaping to Highway 12 east of the town of Escalante, although it is certainly possible to follow the route backward if you're so inclined.

GETTING THERE: Depending on the route you choose to access and escape from Death Hollow, there are three trailheads we recommend using.

Boulder Mail Trailhead (outside Boulder): From Boulder, drive 4.5 miles west toward Escalante on Highway 12, then turn right on Devil's Backbone Road. After about 100 yards, take your first left turn down an unmarked dirt road. In 0.25 mile you will cross the Boulder Airstrip and another 0.25 mile will put you at the signed Boulder Mail Trailhead.

Like Hades, water flows through Death Hollow.

Dip to defend against poison ivy.

Escalante River Trailhead (Highway 12 bridge crossing): From Escalante, drive 14.5 miles east on Highway 12 toward Boulder. Drive over the bridge spanning the Escalante River and make your immediate left into the signed Escalante River Trailhead.

From Boulder, drive 14 miles west on Highway 12 toward Escalante. Just before the bridge spanning the Escalante River, turn right into the signed Escalante River Trailhead.

Upper Escalante River Trailhead (outside Escalante): On the east side of Escalante, look for signs for the Upper Escalante River Trailhead, and turn north off of Highway 12 toward the cemetery. Stay right and continue down the dirt road for about 0.5 mile before turning left. Another 0.5 mile or so and you will arrive.

THE ROUTE: Follow the Boulder Mail Trail for approximately 5.5 miles (see Hike #8, page 99), where a sweeping and distinct panoramic view marks the start of the steep descent into Death Hollow—as do a series of cairns. Follow the mark-

Dropping into Death Hollow.

ers that trend north along the canyon's eastern walls, and find your way down to the cool creek below.

Your first steps into the canyon floor will be directly into the creek, and your feet will not be dry again for the remainder of your outing. Your passage will also cross in and out of the creek through calf cramp-inducing sand, and yes, poison ivy for the next 7 miles through Death Hollow. It is best to accept this as your destiny and forge ahead—tomorrow isn't promised anyway and maybe you are one of the lucky folks immune to the plant's itch-inducing oils.

Fortunately, your destiny also involves crystal pools of water (deep enough for swimming on warm days), miniature waterfalls, wildflowers depending on the season, and sheer cliffs that draw your gaze upward (so don't trip on the melon-sized stones immersed in the water underfoot).

Death Hollow ends at its unimpressive confluence with the Escalante River. At many times of the year, the Escalante is completely dry this far up, and doesn't have reliable water until Mamie Creek and Death Hollow join from the north. If you are heading back to the town of Escalante, turn west at

Walls close in around a poison jungle and shallow waterways.

Poison ivy: The demon of Death Hollow.

the confluence and hike up the Escalante River into town. A better and more enjoyable option is to continue downriver, following the Escalante to where it crosses Highway 12 east of town. Keep an eye out for the arch, ancient Fremont structures, and the natural bridge, all located in the vicinity of Sand Creek and its confluence with the Escalante. Another 2.0 miles will put you at the highway, and hopefully your shuttle donkey.

N
6000
CR 053-86
Durffey Mesa
Durffey Mesa
The Hogback
6160 Pictograph
Escalante River Trailhead
.1 mi
Boulder
Sugarloaf
Hell's Backbone Rd.
Boulder Mail Trailhead
12
12
McGath
Sand Creek
Natural Arch & Ruins
Main Benchmark
Escalante Natural Bridge
Mamie Natural Bridge
Death Hollow
Upper Escalante River Trail
Mail Trail
15.0 mi
Boulder
Box Death Hollow South
Box Death Hollow West
Escalante Natural Bridge
Escalante Trailhead
Escalante Trailhead
12
Escalante
FR 153
Reservoir Road
5 miles
4
3
2
1
0

10. Phipps Arch and Maverick Natural Bridge

DISTRICT:	Canyons of the Escalante/Highway 12
RATING:	Moderate
DISTANCE:	8 miles
ELEVATION GAIN:	800 feet
ROUND-TRIP TIME:	3–6 hours
MAP:	Trails Illustrated #710, Canyons of the Escalante
NEAREST LANDMARK:	Escalante River

COMMENT: The mark of human history lines this hiking route despite the focal point being the geological wonders of Phipps Arch and Maverick Natural Bridge. Almost immediately after leaving the trailhead note the ancient Fremont structure tucked into the cliff wall. Afterward, you'll pass by two modern private residences, which provide a striking contrast. Beyond the section along the river, Phipps Wash (and the accompanying arch) are named for cattle rancher,

A deadly business deal memorialized in stone.
Choose yer partners wisely.

Washington Phipps, who was shot by his business partner, John Boynton, in 1878. By the time you arrive at Phipps Arch, you'll feel far away from modern human life despite never being more than a few miles from Highway 12 at any given moment.

Ancient Fremont structures tower over modern private residencies.

The hike itself meanders in and out of the Escalante River (be prepared for seasonal water level variation and poison ivy) before heading up the dry Phipps Wash. For those with a knack for class 2-3 scrambling and simple route finding, the clamber up to Phipps Arch and surrounding sandstone domes offers stunning views. Maverick Natural Bridge is also a slight detour from Phipps Wash down a side drainage. The extra steps and effort are worth it—you'll be back on the pavement and in your vehicle far too soon anyway. This hike has multiple stream crossings, so prepare for wet feet. The couple of miles around the trailhead are private property, so stay on trail and respect the homeowners.

GETTING THERE: From Escalante, drive 14.5 miles east on Highway 12 toward Boulder. Drive over the bridge spanning the Escalante River and make your immediate left into the signed Escalante River Trailhead.

From Boulder, drive 14 miles west on Highway 12 toward Escalante. Just before the bridge spanning the Escalante River, turn right into the signed Escalante River Trailhead.

THE ROUTE: From the trailhead, cross the highway and find your way to the trail by the bridge. The trail passes by a Fre-

Escalante waterfront property.

mont Structure about 50 feet up on the left then continues on the north bank for a while. You will likely see huge piles of recently cut Russian Olive trees that the BLM, the Escalante River Watershed Partnership, and wild-vigilante-invasive-tree-annihilators-gone-rogue have been attempting to eradicate from the area for years. The first mile or so goes through private property so you should attempt to stay on the obvious and relatively maintained trail that crosses this section. Once through the private property, the trail will cross to the south bank and continue downstream.

You will soon come to a big open meadow and an obvious tree-laden riparian wash coming in on the right. This is Phipps Wash. Enter the wash and head upcanyon. Less than 1.0 mile up, Maverick Wash will come in on the right and it's a quick out-and-back side trip up to the natural bridge.

Back at Phipps Wash, continue upcanyon for 0.25 mile or so until a canyon comes in from the left, which provides access to the arch. The route up is neither well marked nor obvious, and you will need to be fairly comfortable with steep slick-rock and easy scrambling to find your way up to the arch. If the idea of using your hands on a hike doesn't appeal to you then it's best to stop here. The route up is usually laden with cairns, and keep an eye out for stacked rocks helping with gaining the slickrock benches up above. The route is never very difficult, so if you find yourself doing something dangerous, you are probably off route. Once at the arch, it is worth exploring the many nooks and crannies of the rim that you just climbed. Return back to Phipps Wash and back to your car, or for those looking for a longer day you can keep heading upcanyon, eventually exiting at Spencer Flat Road.

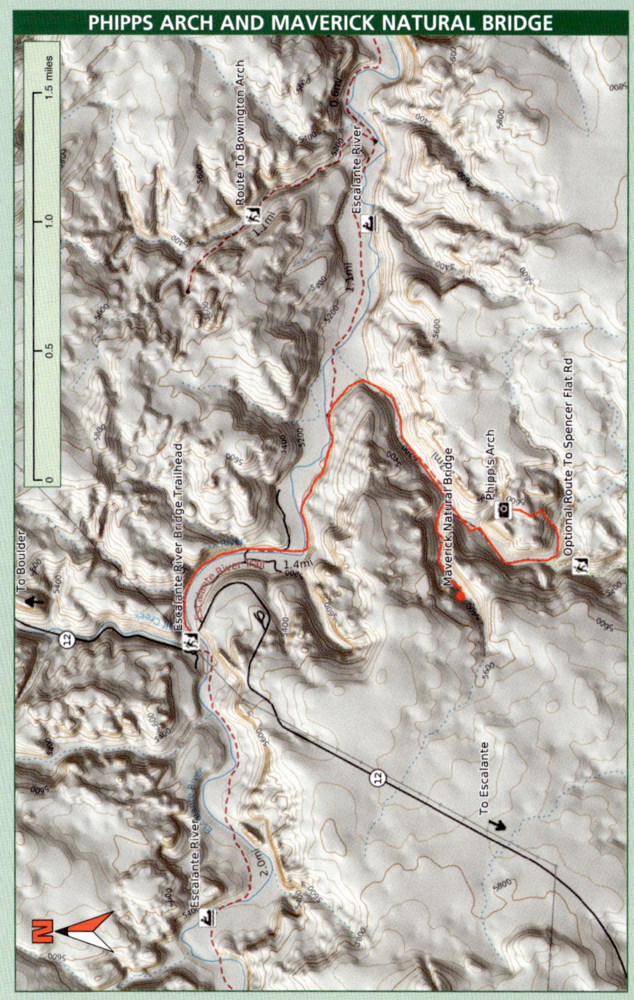
1.5 miles
1.0
0.5
0
Route To Bowington Arch
0.6 mi
Escalante River
1.1 mi
Escalante River
1.3 mi
To Boulder
12
Mill Creek
Escalante River Bridge Trailhead
Escalante River Trail
1.4 mi
Escalante River
Escalante River
2.0 mi
Maverick Natural Bridge
1 mi
Phipp's Arch
Optional Route To Spencer Flat Rd
12
To Escalante
N

11. Bighorn Canyon

DISTRICT:	Canyons of the Escalante/Highway 12
RATING:	Moderate
DISTANCE:	9 miles
ELEVATION GAIN:	1,200 feet
ROUND-TRIP TIME:	3–8 hours
MAP:	Trails Illustrated #710, Canyons of the Escalante
NEAREST LANDMARK:	Escalante River

COMMENT: Walking between the colorful and uniquely textured walls of Bighorn Canyon feels like being in an art gallery. Watch your step (there are a few minor dryfalls and obstacles to negotiate) as you admire the swirls, stripes, and speckles of yellow, pink, red, orange, white, and burgundy that adorn the canyon as well as the sandstone towers and formations that line the canyon rim.

The canyon itself is a tributary of Harris Wash, making it possible to use this route to connect Highway 12 with Hole-

Ancient art gallery.

In-The-Rock Road (although this route recommends turning back when you reach the wash).

This canyon is typically dry, so hike prepared with your own water supplies.

Swirling Sands of Color: A Bighorn Canyon original masterpiece.

GETTING THERE: From Escalante, drive east on Highway 12 for 10.5 miles. Just before the hairpin turn, turn right onto the unmarked dirt road. This is Spencer Flat Road. Drive exactly 2.0 miles and park at the large campsite on the rim of the canyon, overlooking the Escalante Canyons to the northeast.

From Boulder, drive west on Highway 12 for 18 miles. Just after a hairpin turn, turn left onto Spencer Flat Road and follow the directions above.

THE ROUTE: There are many entry and exit points for Bighorn Canyon. The route here is a recommended option, although one could certainly hike any of the many head and side canyons that make up the area collectively referred to as Bighorn Canyon.

From the parking area, drop down into the canyon to the south, and simply follow the canyon down. There are a number of large dryfalls you will have to navigate around both on the hike downcanyon, as well as the return up the west fork, but all are easily bypassed with just a bit of route finding. After a couple miles you will arrive at a large confluence with what is generally accepted to be Bighorn Canyon. Continuing down, the canyon narrows up almost all the way to its confluence with its West Fork, and a few hundred yards more to its confluence with Harris Wash. Once at Harris, turn around and head left up the West Fork. The really interesting parts

The Bighorn Canyon Art Walk.

Texture: An exhibit in full sensory activation.

of the West Fork are all within the first mile, so doing a short out and back up this fork, then returning the way you came is a nice option. Another option here is to just continue up the West Fork until the canyon opens up to the plateau above and the western rim of the canyon that you hiked down. This cross-country route simply trends north, and slightly east when possible, edging along the rim of the canyon until you hit Spencer Flat Road, and back to the parking area and your vehicle.

This hike is also occasionally accessed via Hole-In-The-Rock Road where Harris Wash crosses (see map).

To Escalante
To Boulder
Mamie Benchmark
12
12
Spencer Flat Road
P
Spencer Flat Road
Optional Rim Route
3.9mi
3.8mi
Bighorn Canyon
4.9mi
West Fork
To Escalante
Harris Wash Parking
1.9mi
Hole-In-The-Rock Rd
Harris Wash
0   0.5   1.0   1.5   2.0 miles
N

12. Lower Calf Creek Falls

DISTRICT:	Canyons of the Escalante/Highway 12
RATING:	Easy
DISTANCE:	6 miles
ELEVATION GAIN:	Negligible
ROUND-TRIP TIME:	2–3 hours
MAP:	Trails Illustrated #710, Canyons of the Escalante
NEAREST LANDMARK:	The Hogback

COMMENT: Surely one of the most popular hikes in GSENM, this highly used trail satisfies many a tourist's desire to get out and see towering canyons, lush riparian zones, and a giant year-round waterfall with a killer swimming hole. Its ease of access and easy terrain make this a great quick stop if passing through, and a good summer hike as there is plenty of water, although you may have to keep your trousers on as this is a family friendly place. If swimming in the nude is your thing, check out the Upper Falls (Hike #14, page 124) or head on up

The marquis roadside hike of Grand Staircase-Escalante National Monument.

Keep your head up.

Precious desert water.

to Boulder where that kind of behavior is tolerated.

GETTING THERE: From Escalante, head east on Highway 12 toward Boulder. Drive 19 miles, over the Escalante River bridge, and turn left at the heavily signed Lower Calf Creek Falls Recreation Area.

From Boulder, head west on Highway 12 toward Escalante. Drive 9 miles, passing over The Hogback, and turn right at the heavily signed Lower Calf Creek Falls Recreation Area.

We dare you to keep your clothes on.

THE ROUTE: Starting at the trailhead, head upcanyon for 3.0 miles until you arrive at the falls. Return the way you came.

N
0.9mi
Durffey Mesa
To Boulder
McGath Point
Calf Creek
12
Lower Calf Creek Falls
6000
0.6mi
6000
Lower Calf Creek Falls Trailhead
Peak 6160 Pictograph Point
12
Escalante River Bridge & Trailhead
Escalante River
2.0mi
0.4mi
1.1mi
Escalante River 0.6mi
0.1mi
To Escalante
1.7mi
0   1   2   3 miles

13. Upper Calf Creek Falls

DISTRICT:	Canyons of the Escalante/Highway 12
RATING:	Moderate
DISTANCE:	2.3 miles
ELEVATION GAIN:	600 feet
ROUND-TRIP TIME:	1–2 hours
MAP:	Trails Illustrated #710, Canyons of the Escalante
NEAREST LANDMARK:	The Hogback

COMMENT: It's a mistake to assume Upper Calf Creek Falls is less interesting or less beautiful simply because it is less popular than Lower Calf Creek Falls. In fact, that is a major part of its appeal. Oh, and don't forget the stunning 126-foot waterfall. Unlike Lower Calf Creek Falls further downstream that begins at a paved parking lot and follows a well-marked, maintained trail, Upper Calf Creek Falls has no marked signs on the highway, is exposed, and strenuous. This short,

An oasis within the geography of hope.

steep hike on mostly slickrock offers incredible views of the surrounding region before diving down into the canyon that houses Calf Creek (beware the lurking poison ivy). Yes, this hike is a small bite of what you are looking for on a real desert outing. For those who like to explore, it is possible to follow a route upward to the head of the falls where several smaller falls and swimming holes are located.

Be like the water, moving through the landscape and falling in love as you kiss the stone ground.

GETTING THERE: From Escalante: Head east on Highway 12 for 21 miles and turn left onto the unsigned pullout. There is a trail marker and sign.

From Boulder: Head west on Highway 12 for 7 miles and turn right onto the unsigned pullout for the trailhead.

THE ROUTE: From the trailhead, take the worn path to where the steep slickrock slab begins and follow the cairns until the route levels off onto a bench. From here take the single-track trail to continue around the rim as you gently descend toward the lower reaches of the canyon. As you near the falls the route will split—take the lower route heading down to the falls.

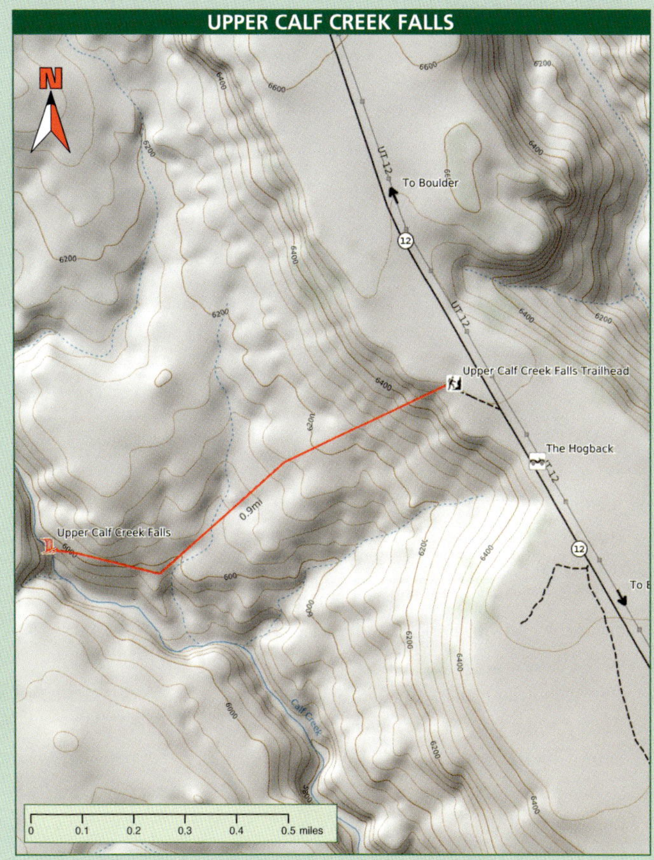

To Boulder
12
Ut 12
Ut 12
Upper Calf Creek Falls Trailhead
The Hogback
12
To B
Upper Calf Creek Falls
0.9mi
Calf Creek
6600
6200
6400
6200
6400
6200
6200
6400
6200
6400
6400
6200
6400
6200
6400
6000
6200
6400
600
600
600
6200
6200
6600
6600
N
0   0.1   0.2   0.3   0.4   0.5 miles

14. Upper Escalante River Trail

DISTRICT:	Canyons of the Escalante/Highway 12
RATING:	Easy
DISTANCE:	13 miles
ELEVATION CHANGE:	750 feet
ROUND-TRIP TIME:	Full day
MAP:	Trails Illustrated #710, Canyons of the Escalante
NEAREST LANDMARK:	Escalante River

COMMENT: The lower water levels of the Upper Escalante River Trail make this an excellent way to experience the region's premier waterway without the trudgery (drudgery of trudging) of hiking through the deeper and obstacle-strewn true river miles beginning after Highway 12. Done as a car shuttle, this route begins in the town of Escalante and travels downriver through towering Navajo Sandstone walls to end at the Escalante River (The Bridge) Trailhead. Noteworthy side trips to consider are Death Hollow (with the Escalante River being one of its few entrance and exit points) and Sand Creek. The star attractions of this route appear in its final miles—a natural arch (12.3 miles from the trailhead) and a natural bridge a bit further. Both formations stand on hiker's right heading downriver. Be sure to pay homage to the area's rich pre-history by taking the time to admire the ancient Fremont structure tucked beneath the natural arch. According to archaeologist R.E. Burrillo, the Fremont were, "a semi-sedentary culture that practiced a mixture of maize farming and foraging between about 150 and 1300 BC." After your hike, scramble up to the Hundred Hand Pictograph Wall above the parking lot after crossing the Escalante before hitting the road.

Sandstone and sky framed in rose hues.

GETTING THERE

Escalante River Trailhead (Hwy. 12 bridge crossing): From Escalante, drive 14.5 miles east on Highway 12 toward Boulder. Drive over the bridge spanning the Escalante River and make your immediate left into the signed Escalante River Trailhead.

From Boulder, drive 14 miles west on Highway 12 toward Escalante. Just before the bridge spanning the Escalante River, turn right into the signed Escalante River Trailhead.

Upper Escalante River Trailhead (outside Escalante): On the east side of Escalante, look for signs for the Upper Escalante River Trailhead, and turn north off of Highway 12 toward the cemetery. Stay right and continue down the dirt road for about 0.5 mile before turning left. Another 0.5 mile or so and you will arrive.

THE ROUTE: Most people choose to start in Escalante and walk downcanyon to what is known simply as The Bridge. At many

Lose count of how many times you cross the river.

Bent stone washed in sunlight.

times of the year, the streambed is dry until its confluence with Death Hollow and Mamie Creek about halfway, approximately 7 miles downcanyon from the start. Simply navigate your way downcanyon, explore side canyons if the urge overwhelms you, and go swimming in the Death Hollow narrows. A couple of miles from the bridge, look for an impressive natural arch on the right, and an equally impressive set of ancient structures. The Escalante Natural Bridge is just a bit farther downcanyon, and if time permits, explore Sand Creek Canyon as it joins from the north. The (modern) house on the cliff marks your arrival at The Bridge. Cross the river one last time and you have arrived at the trailhead. If you arranged a shuttle then get it here, or bike, ride your burro, or hitch back to town.

The Hogback
UT 12
UT 12
McGath Point
Sand Creek
Mamie Natural Bridge
Death Hollow
Escalante Natural Bridge
Escalante Arch & Ruins
Natural Arch & Ruins
Escalante River Trailhead
Marble Benchmark
Upper Escalante River Trail
Escalante Trailhead
Mail Trail
Box-Death Hollow South Ridge
Boulder
Escalante
Pine Creek Road
5 miles

15. Escalante Lookout Trail and Micro Death Hollow

DISTRICT:	Canyons of the Escalante/Highway 12
RATING:	Easy, difficult if including Micro Death Hollow
DISTANCE:	2-3 miles round trip
ELEVATION GAIN:	500 feet
ROUND-TRIP TIME:	1–3 hours
MAP:	Trails Illustrated #710, Canyons of the Escalante
NEAREST LANDMARK:	Escalante River

COMMENT: The Escalante Lookout Trail is a great option for those with a short amount of time and looking for an easy, short hike close to town. The trail follows the western rim of a side canyon locally referred to as "Micro Death Hollow," given its proximity to the much more popular Death Hollow, which joins the Escalante River from the north about 1.0 mile upcanyon. The Lookout Trail ends at a point offering panoramic views of the Escalante watershed in all directions.

Lookout into the wide vistas of Escalante from above its tightest corridor.

For those looking for a bit more action and hoping to get your slot on, you can navigate down the slickrock expanse and back up the canyon you have been paralleling from the start.

Micro-dose on the local Death Hollow fascination— this just might be the tightest squeeze of your life! The slot canyon itself is quite short, but be prepared to move slowly as you literally slide, pull, chimney and suck in your gut to get through the tall and narrow

A tiny taste of death.

walls that are only inches apart at points. For some, passage in the upper narrows will not be possible without stemming off the deck (and don't even attempt it with a pack), and it is certainly not recommended for anyone with claustrophobia. The lower sections are more open and friendly with swirling mazes carved into the rock underfoot. The descent into the canyon requires route finding (although this mainly pertains to selective footing as the direction to Micro Death Hollow is obvious). A brief bit of Class 3 scrambling is also required to descend into the canyon.

GETTING THERE: From Escalante, head east on Highway 12 toward Boulder. Drive about 7.0 miles, passing Hole-In-The-Rock Road, and turn left on an unmarked dirt road between mile markers 66 and 67. Drive due north toward the rim of the Escalante for about 1.5 miles until you arrive at the parking area perched high on the rim above Micro Death Hollow.

THE ROUTE: From the parking area, head due north staying high on the western rim of Micro Death Hollow. There is a

Mo micro-dosing.

relatively easy-to-follow footpath that takes you the full mile to the lookout on the rim of the Escalante Canyon. You can either head back to your car from here after taking in the views, or continue the adventure down into the canyon you have been hiking beside. From the lookout on the Escalante, find the easiest way down to the slickrock; you may have to backtrack a bit to find an easy enough route. Once down, aim toward the confluence of Micro Death Hollow and the Escalante River, choosing the lowest angle, safest route along the sea of Navajo slickrock. The route to the canyon floor comes in just above the confluence, as there are impassable dryfalls at the lowest part of Micro Death Hollow. Find the 3rd class scramble down to the canyon floor. From here you can check out the 100 yards or so downcanyon to the dryfall, or head upcanyon, arriving quickly at the narrows. Squeeze between the walls upcanyon as far as your body will allow. For skinny canyoneers this will be easier, and your hike won't end until the almost 300-foot dryfall near the head of the canyon. From here the only way out is the way you came, so suck it back in and retrace your steps all the way back to the rim, and eventually your vehicle.

ESCALANTE LOOKOUT TRAIL AND MICRO DEATH HOLLOW

16. The Gulch/ King Bench Canyon

DISTRICT:	Canyons of the Escalante/Burr Trail
RATING:	Difficult
DISTANCE:	11–26 miles
ELEVATION GAIN:	Varies
ROUND-TRIP TIME:	1–4 days
MAP:	Trails Illustrated #710, Canyons of the Escalante
NEAREST LANDMARK:	Burr Trail Road

COMMENT: If your desert-loving blood craves the thickening effects of dehydration, your skin cracked like the crypto crust you avoid walking on, and you use mud as your preferred source of sun protection—head to The Gulch. This is a hike for true desert aficionados, for it is hiking through the most challenging aspects of this area's terrain simply for its own sake. Long sandy washes, mud-filled slot canyons (that require extensive re-routing), constant whacking through thorny brush, a lack of water until you reach the Escalante River, and then the torture of once again leaving it behind— the only way out is back through!

For those willing to endure, there is incredible beauty tucked within The Gulch, and endless exploration and options to extend your hike. King Bench Canyon, a colorful and shapely slot, is a worthwhile side trip (and also one of the few sources of water before the Escalante). For those not interested in an out and back, King Bench is also a noteworthy exit route, although complete self-navigation and route finding is necessary. When done properly, you will enjoy views across the top of the canyons all the way to the Straight

Looking into the gut of The Gulch.

Cliffs, and avoid getting cliffed out, before returning to The Gulch for the final miles back to your vehicle.

The Gulch is a very popular spot for grazing cattle. Don't be surprised if you encounter these subsidized beasts, their endless trail meanderings, or their ornery owners.

Water is available on this hike, but be prepared for long stretches between sources. Varied levels of route finding and cross-country travel are found within The Gulch depending on the route you select.

The nearby Upper Gulch Trail is another noteworthy consideration while you are in this zone.

GETTING THERE: From the west side of Boulder, Utah, turn south on the scenic Burr Trail Road. Go 10 miles, and just before bottoming out the long switchback above The Gulch, turn right at the signed pullout for the Lower Gulch Trailhead.

Self-reflection not your thing? The canyons will have you face yourself in all directions.

Hone your will to wade.

THE ROUTE: From the parking area, head south for 0.25 mile until you reach the main Gulch drainage. Find the largest and most well-worn footpath (probably a cow trail) and start hiking south through a thick riparian zone choked with cow pies. After 5.0 miles you will arrive at the confluence of King Bench Canyon. About 0.25 mile up this canyon you will find clear water, and it's the only reliable water source north of the Narrows that has not been tainted by cattle.

From here, hikers can choose to hike up King Bench Canyon, exploring the many sections of narrows before dead-ending at a large dryfall a couple of miles upcanyon. There is a bypass route on the east rim of King Bench (hard to find), if one wanted to use this as an exit route to get back to the trailhead.

If King Bench Canyon isn't your destination, continue on downcanyon. Within a couple of miles the walls begin to close in and form narrows. The canyon continues its relatively narrow character for 0.5 mile or so, before

Refill your water supply and splash around at the Escalante confluence.

turning sharply left toward the east and dropping off into a proper slot canyon often filled with deep pools of chilly water. From here, you have a few options.

To continue downcanyon uninterrupted, one must downclimb the boulder jam at the top of the slot. This is possible with a couple of tricky stemming moves and a fist jam under the large boulder, but depending on the level of the water below you, you will probably have to eventually drop into the pool and swim downcanyon briefly to access

Slot swimming.

dry land. Once you drop, you are committed to going downcanyon so make sure this is what you want to do before making the move. A 20-foot rope here would help immensely, not only with the descent, but if you want to return the same way.

Beware of rolling stones.

Log jam session in King Bench Canyon.

If none of the above sounds particularly fun to you, there is another option. Turn around and hike back upcanyon. Before the end of the narrow section, keep an eye out on the left (west) wall. A downed oak tree trunk lies up against a slickrock slope that is easily climbable. This is the start of the narrows bypass route. This junction is heavily marked with cairns, as well as the entire bypass route, but as we all know, cairns fall, get blown over, wash away, and get knocked down, so now would be a reasonable time to turn on your navigational and route finding skills. Climb the slickrock slope following cairns to the top of the bench on the western rim of The Gulch. Follow the rim south and then east, bending with the canyon as you bypass the slot canyon and the drop you didn't feel like plunging down. Follow the trail down a bench, and when the canyon bends right again, locate the crack in the wall that allows reasonably easy access down to the canyon floor. Remember where this enters the canyon as it will also act as your escape route on the return journey.

From here, either head back upcanyon to explore the slot, or continue downcanyon toward the Escalante River. A couple hundred yards after reaching the canyon bottom from the bypass route, you will see a small canyon joining from the north. This is Halfway Hollow--a cul-de-sac of a side canyon that dead-ends at a grotto with a large dryfall and "relatively" clean water. Halfway Hollow can be explored further by bypassing this point on the rim, but we will leave that for another day.

The next few miles down to the Escalante sees little traffic. The cows can't get past the slot, and few take on the bushwhacky slog down to the Escalante. Those that do will appreciate the isolation and the swim upon arrival at the river. This last section is usually only done by backpackers looking to access the Escalante (also

A creative solution to obstacles in King Bench Canyon.

Taking The Gulch in stride.

King Bench Canyon narrows.   Get lost inside the earth.

ideal for a water resupply) and link with another canyon either up or downstream.

From the river, drag yourself out of the water and trudge back up the few miles to Halfway Hollow and the narrows bypass route. Regardless of how you get there, continue upcanyon until you arrive at the King Bench Canyon confluence. If at this point you are cursing the canyon deities and sick of the hot spots on your hips, simply continue plodding back up The Gulch and to your car. Those looking for a little more can continue up King Bench Canyon, locate the narrows bypass route on the east side of the canyon, and figure out the cross-country route back to the minor side drainage to re-access The Gulch about 1.0 mile or so south of the trailhead. This latter option requires excellent navigational and route-finding skills, scrambling, and remarkable patience while continually being forced to retreat at cliff's edge. As such, this option isn't highly recommended.

Once back at the trailhead, have yourself a cold beer, and go get a fancy burger in Boulder.

THE GULCH/KING BENCH CANYON
Durffey Mesa
Burr Trail Rd
King Bench
CR 0598
Burr Trail Rd
To Boulder
Durffey Mesa
CR 0598
Lower Gulch Trailhead
6000
Peak 6157
King Bench Canyon Route (Approximate)
Peak 6209
Peak 6160 Pictograph
Lower Gulch Trail
Halfway Hollow
1.1mi
Narrows Bypass Route -->
1.7mi
N
Escalante River
0   1   2   3   4   5 miles

17. Little Death Hollow/Wolverine Petrified Forest Loop

DISTRICT:	Canyons of the Escalante/Burr Trail
RATING:	Difficult
DISTANCE:	About 20 miles (23 miles if not using a car shuttle)
ELEVATION CHANGE:	800 feet
ROUND-TRIP TIME:	1–2 days
MAP:	Trails Illustrated #710, Canyons of the Escalante
NEAREST LANDMARK:	Burr Trail Road

COMMENT: This lively hike with a scary name takes you through some of the most unique terrain in Grand Staircase-Escalante National Monument. The narrow slotted passageways of Little Death Hollow lead you to a splash in the Escalante, before an easy cruise through Horse Canyon (basically a jeep road) and then the petrified wood forest of Wolverine Canyon where fossilized ferns can still be seen on

Walk through the endangered Circle Cliffs.

the walls. Both canyons and the Circle Cliffs comprise Wingate Sandstone, which is more resistant to erosion (the type of rock that likes to be climbed!) and much more rare than the typical Navajo Sandstone that most slot canyons are formed from.

While Little Death Hollow and the Wolverine Canyon certainly qualify as separate routes when done as out-and-backs, their conveniently located trailheads (only 3 miles apart) make this an enjoyable loop even without a car shuttle.

This route includes an out-and-back to the Escalante River (adding approximately 4.0 miles total), both for a reliable resupply of water and the always-fun way to break up a long hike: with a swim!

GETTING THERE: From the west side of Boulder, turn south on the scenic Burr Trail Road. Go 18.4 miles via this enjoyable drive and keep an eye out for a sign pointing the way to Horse, Wolverine, and Little Death Hollow trailheads. This is the Wolverine Loop Road.

Tunnel vision.

The walls are closing in again.

Grotesque walls of imagination.   Surreal Dalí-esque formations.

Stay left at the first junction (going right will take you down the controversial road within Horse Canyon). After 10 miles from the Burr Trail Road turnoff, you will arrive at the Wolverine Canyon Trailhead. If you are able, drop a shuttle (car, bike, or mule) here, and continue another 2.5 miles to the signed Little Death Hollow Trailhead.

*** WARNING:** Wolverine Loop Road is a rarely maintained dirt road that crosses washes with deep sand. High clearance is recommended during even the driest of days. The road is even at times impassable to Off Highway Vehicles (OHVs), especially if what was a dry sandy wash becomes a rushing wall of mud and boulders during a monsoon.

THE ROUTE: Little Death Hollow begins below the Circle Cliffs, bordering a significant geological area no longer within the monument boundaries. Follow the boot-beaten path through the canyon, and watch the walls begin to nar-

Wingate likes to be climbed.

row and tighten into a true slot canyon. The first interesting section will require you to either downclimb around a large boulder jam into the pool of water where the canyon drops off, or scramble up above the water and traverse a bench in the canyon for a few hundred feet before downclimbing back to the canyon floor. From here it is pretty much inevitable that you will walk through water and mud. It is 8.0 total miles from the trailhead to the junction with Horse Canyon.

Follow Horse Canyon downstream for 2.0 miles until you reach the confluence of the Escalante. Fill up with water here, and then return to the junction of Horse Creek and Little Death Hollow. From here continue up Horse Canyon, mostly along an uninteresting jeep road, which on a positive note makes for a quicker pace.

Approximately 2.0 miles along Horse Canyon the entrance to Wolverine will be on the right. It is the first major canyon confluence north of Little Death Hollow. It is unmarked, but where the giant wash of Horse Canyon splits, take the wash

Recharging at the confluence.

The Circle Cliffs face an unknown future.

to the right. You will be greeted with walls of gnarled and cavernous sandstone, which appear to be ancient entrance gates to otherworldly destinations. Lacking the narrow passages of its neighboring canyon cousins, what Little Death Hollow lacks in "slotiness" is more than made up by its mind-bending Dali-esque melting walls of red and black sandstone, offering Alice in Wonderland-type structures and grotesque walls of imagination. This zone was wet, subtropical, and near the equator during the Late Triassic Period (225 million years ago), and home to lush ferns (whose marks still remain fossilized on the canyon walls nearest to the river), giant conifers, and dinosaurs.

Follow the canyon for 3.0 miles until you reach a fork in the stream, where you will trend right around the sandstone tower–crowned butte. Continue 2.0 miles cross-country until you arrive where your mule is napping. If not using a mule or shuttle, continue down the road for 2.5 miles to the Little Death Hollow Trailhead.

LITTLE DEATH HOLLOW/WOLVERINE PETRIFIED FOREST LOOP
N
To Burr Trail and Boulder
Wolverine Loop Rd.
Wolverine Canyon Trailhead
Wolverine Loop Rd.
Horse Canyon
CR 0-601
Little Death Hollow Trailhead
6000
6000
6000
6000
6000
6000
Escalante River
5981
Escalante River
5932
Gle
Glen C
6000
Glen Canyon National Recreation Area
0   1   2   3   4   5 miles

18. Round Valley Draw

DISTRICT:	Grand Staircase/Cottonwood Canyon Road
RATING:	Moderate
DISTANCE:	3–6 miles
ELEVATION GAIN:	300 feet
ROUND-TRIP TIME:	2–5 hours
MAP:	Trails Illustrated #714, Grand Staircase Paunsaugunt Plateau
NEAREST LANDMARK:	Grosvenor Arch

COMMENT: Round Valley Draw showcases colorful and shapely Navajo Sandstone, with a few moderately technical pour-overs and boulder sections to descend into this narrow, high-walled slot canyon. Take note that this route will require some basic scrambling and descents and hikers may consider utilizing a rope for gaining access to the slot. There are two optional exit routes on faint trails on the west rim of the canyon that will take you back to the trail that precedes

Let your way find you.

the actual Round Valley Draw. Experience and comfort with route finding are recommended for this exit. For most, it is best to plan to return to the trailhead via the same route in the canyon, and again some basic scrambling techniques will be necessary.

Light creeps into Round Valley Draw.

GETTING THERE: From Escalante, drive west on Highway 12 for approximately 34 miles. Head south onto Kodachrome Road/Main Street, keeping an eye out for Kodachrome State Park signs. Reset your odometer here. In about 2.5 miles, the road will change to Cottonwood Canyon Road. At approximately 14 miles, turn right onto the marked access road to Round Valley Draw. Go for about 1.5 miles until you reach the trailhead and the BLM registry.

You can also access this hike from the south via Page, Arizona, or Kanab, Utah. From Page, head west on Highway 89 (26 miles), or from Kanab, head east on Highway 89 (41 miles). Both arrive at the turnoff for Cottonwood Canyon Road, where you will drive north about 32 miles until the signed turnoff for Round Valley Draw.

THE ROUTE: From the parking area, follow the well-defined single-track that parallels and crosses a sandy wash several times. In less than a mile you will come to a large pine tree and some cairns indicating where to begin your descent into the canyon to the opening of the slot. The entrance to Round Valley Draw itself looks more intimidating and steep than it actually is (approximately 15 feet). If you are nervous about

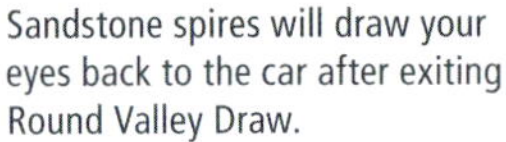

Sandstone spires will draw your eyes back to the car after exiting Round Valley Draw.

Sunlight above the depths of Round Valley Draw.

the descent, have more experienced scramblers enter first so that they can spot you at the bottom. Another option is to throw a rope, but given the excellent hand and foot holds, this is unnecessary for most hikers. Look for handholds on the left when facing toward the canyon.

Once on the canyon floor, the narrow walls tower above the mostly sandy bottom. The canyon widens considerably at its confluence with another, around 3.0 miles, marking the point for your turnaround, or the optional exit route (see map). It is also possible to continue hiking downcanyon to the confluence with Hackberry Canyon, and onward from there for those looking for a longer outing.

The optional exit route can also be used as access to Lower Round Valley Draw from a different access road off Cottonwood Canyon Road. This is a good option for those not comfortable with the initial descent into Round Valley Draw, but still wish to see the canyon.

ROUND VALLEY DRAW
N
Cottonwood Canyon Rd
Upper Slickrock
To Hwy 12
Lower Slickrock
To Hwy 89
Trailhead
Optional Exit Route
Round Valley Draw
2.3mi
Optional Exit Route
To Hackberry Canyon
0
0.5
1.0
1.5 miles

19. Yellow Rock

DISTRICT:	Grand Staircase/Cottonwood Canyon Road
RATING:	Difficult
DISTANCE:	2.5 miles round trip
ELEVATION GAIN:	750 feet
ROUND-TRIP TIME:	1–3 hours
MAP:	Trails Illustrated #714, Grand Staircase Paunsaugunt Plateau
NEAREST LANDMARK:	The Cockscomb

COMMENT: Click the heels of your hiking boots together and say, "There's no place like Grand Staircase-Escalante National Monument!" Though this hike is only 1.0 mile long each way, plan plenty of time to wander and explore this giant color-and-texture-strewn dome of Navajo Sandstone with sweeping views of the Cockscomb, Lower Hackberry, and the surrounding region.

Don't let the short distance fool you—this is a strenuous cross-country route on steep, loose, and exposed terrain. There is no water, so bring your own.

Follow the Yellow Rock route.

All the golden lands ahead of you.   A really big rock.

GETTING THERE: From Escalante, drive west on Highway 12 for approximately 34 miles. In Cannonville, head south onto Kodachrome Road/Main Street, keeping an eye out for Kodachrome State Park signs. Reset your odometer here. In about 2.5 miles, the road will change to Cottonwood Canyon Road. At approximately 32 miles, you will park at the marked parking area for Lower Hackberry trailhead.

You can also access this hike from the south via Page, Arizona, or Kanab, Utah. From Page, head west on Highway 89 (26 miles), or from Kanab, head east on Highway 89 (46 miles). Both arrive at the turnoff for Cottonwood Canyon Road, where you will drive north about 14 miles until the marked parking area for Lower Hackberry trailhead.

THE ROUTE: From the trailhead, follow the short boot-beaten path into Cottonwood Wash and go left. Continue down the wash for approximately 0.25 mile (this is past the more obvious path into Lower Hackberry) until you reach the next side canyon with a faint use-path. Follow the tracks that lead to an extremely steep and sandy talus slope, climbing the obvious upward path until you reach a saddle, and continue west across slickrock and sandy drainages toward the base of Yellow Rock. From here you can choose your own adventure—winding along the maze of reds, pinks, and yellows, marching straight up to its summit, or sitting still (to catch your breath) and marvel at what this actually is—a really big yellow rock.

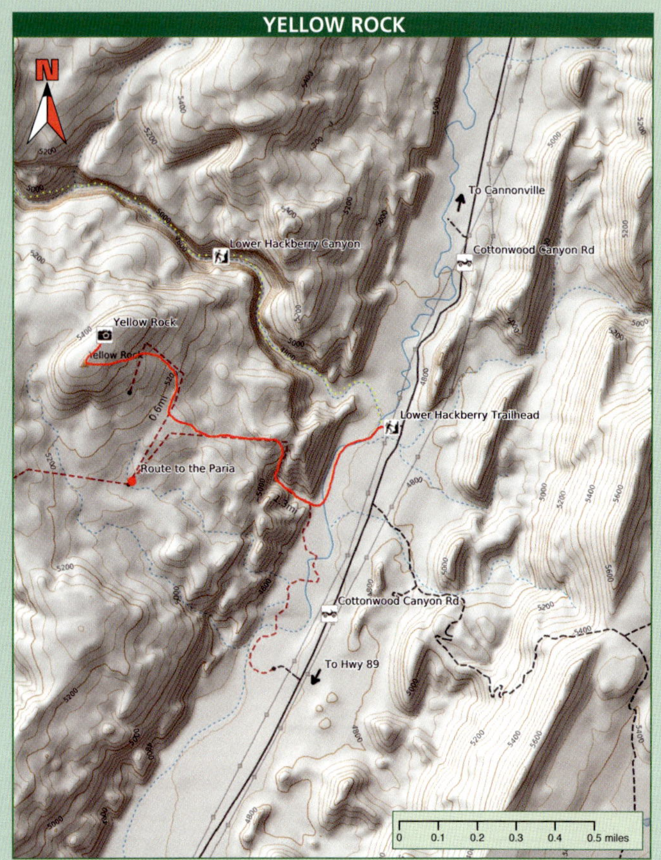

YELLOW ROCK
N
To Cannonville
Cottonwood Canyon Rd
Lower Hackberry Canyon
Yellow Rock
Yellow Rock
Lower Hackberry Trailhead
0.6mi
Route to the Paria
1.3mi
Cottonwood Canyon Rd
To Hwy 89
0   0.1   0.2   0.3   0.4   0.5 miles

20. Cottonwood Narrows

DISTRICT:	Grand Staircase/Cottonwood Canyon Road
RATING:	Easy
DISTANCE:	2–4 miles
ELEVATION GAIN:	Negligible
ROUND-TRIP TIME:	1–3 hours
MAP:	Trails Illustrated #714, Grand Staircase Paunsaugunt Plateau
NEAREST LANDMARK:	Grosvenor Arch

COMMENT: Cottonwood Narrows is short, non-technical hike and an excellent place for hikers of all abilities to enjoy a spectacular slot canyon within Grand Staircase-Escalante. Expect sandy and primarily non-rocky terrain along the canyon floor of the Cottonwood Narrows. Over time,

Cottonwood Creek has artfully carved this passageway in the Navajo Sandstone walls that form the uplift of the Cockscomb. Although this hike is relatively short, water is not available in Cottonwood Creek and temperatures here can scorch (especially May to early October), so hike prepared with your own supply of water.

GETTING THERE: From Escalante, drive west on Highway 12 for approximately 34 miles. In Cannonville, head south onto Kodachrome Road/Main Street, keeping an eye out for Kodachrome State Park signs. Reset your odometer here. In about 2.5 miles, the road will change to Cottonwood Canyon Road. After approximately 21 miles, you will park at the marked parking area for Cottonwood Narrows, South.

You can also access this hike from the south via Page, Arizona, or Kanab, Utah. From Page, head west on Highway 89 (26 miles), or from Kanab, head east on Highway 89 (46 miles). Both arrive at the turnoff for Cottonwood Canyon Road, where you will drive north about 25 miles until the marked parking area for Cottonwood Narrows, South.

THE ROUTE: This route is accessible from both the south and north trailheads and can be completed as an out-and-back or car shuttle (these directions begin at the south trailhead). Cottonwood Narrows is 2.0 miles total from point-to-point but it is possible to continue along the general route for many more miles if you desire a longer hike. From the south trailhead, follow the well-defined single track to the entrance of the canyon. While the canyon starts out wide and sandy, you will quickly need to ascend a series of boulders strewn across the canyon. There is no need to climb or scramble if you navigate this correctly. At just under 1.0 mile the route splits toward another side canyon to the west. Continue on the route as the canyon begins to narrow considerably to form the official "slot" portion of the route.

At approximately 1.7 miles, follow the single-track trail to the north trailhead (if you have a car shuttle) or return along the same route back to the south trailhead. It is also possible to bypass the north trailhead and continue upcanyon and along the creek for additional mileage.

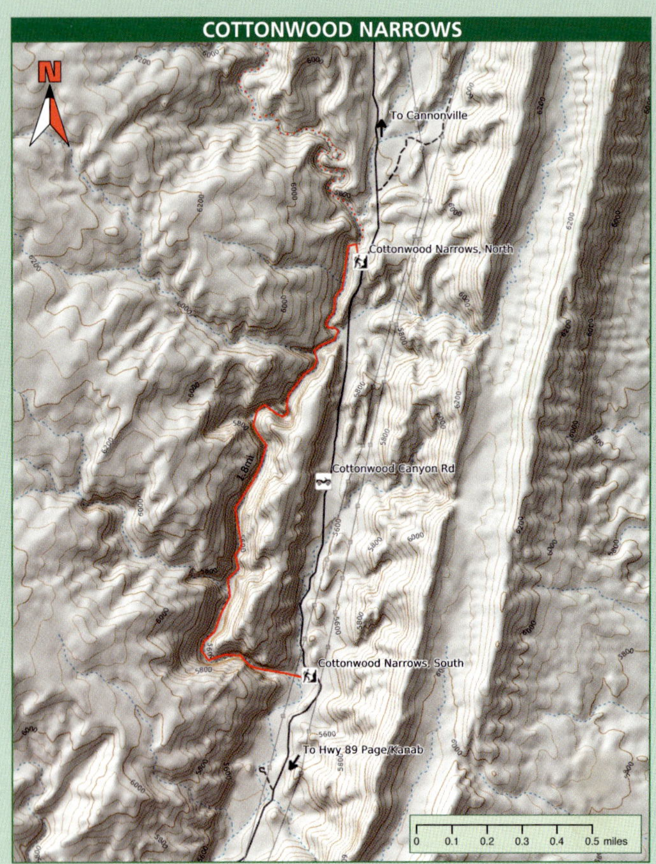
N
To Cannonville
Cottonwood Narrows, North
Cottonwood Canyon Rd
1.8 mi
Cottonwood Narrows, South
To Hwy 89 Page/Kanab
0   0.1   0.2   0.3   0.4   0.5 miles

21. Bull Valley Gorge and Willis Creek Narrows

DISTRICT:	Grand Staircase/Skutumpah Road
RATING:	Difficult
DISTANCE:	16 miles
ELEVATION GAIN:	800 feet
ROUND-TRIP TIME:	1–2 days
MAP:	Trails Illustrated #714, Grand Staircase Paunsaugunt Plateau
NEAREST LANDMARK:	Paria River

COMMENT: In a region brimming with morbid nomenclature—numerous Death Hollows, Devil's Garden, Hell's Backbone—it is quite surprising that Bull Valley Gorge did not earn a name change. There is an old pickup truck wedged and hanging precariously between the narrow walls of Bull Valley Gorge (perhaps better named "Jaws of Death"). The frightening accident occurred in the 1950s when the truck slid off the narrow bridge on Skutumpah Road and into the

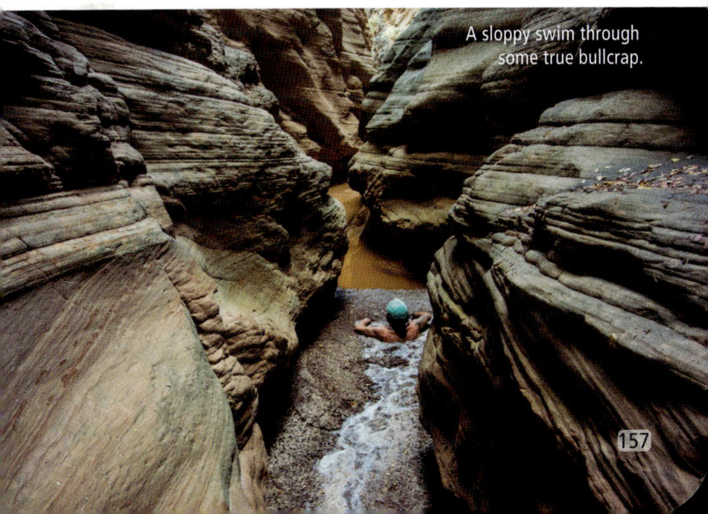
A sloppy swim through some true bullcrap.

Running of the Bull Valley Gorge.   Jaws of Death.

canyon where it remains stuck. Beyond and below this ominous site, easily visible to anyone who parks at the trailhead and walks to the canyon rim, lies a demanding slot canyon that, although is non-technical, will challenge most hiker's sense of adventure.

Bull Valley Gorge requires significant downclimbing, including a 12-foot dryfall. No ropes are necessary, but a certain comfort level and experience with physical slot canyon terrain are imperative. Water and mud are frequently present throughout the gorge, and at certain times of the year the deeper pools will require swimming. Be prepared with extra dry layers and a method to keep anything in your packs dry. A wetsuit is a worthwhile consideration year-round. Even during warm days, hypothermia is a true danger in places like this due to frigid water temperatures, limited sun exposure in the darkest recesses of the canyon, and striking day/night temperature contrasts.

Beyond the Bull Valley Gorge narrows, the route is a pleasant hike along Sheep Creek and up Willis Creek on flat terrain. The Willis Creek Narrows, just a short trek from the Willis Creek Trailhead, ripple with shades of faint orange and streaks of black varnish.

The narrows of Bull Valley Gorge can be avoided simply by making this hike an out-and-back beginning at the Willis Creek Trailhead (turning around whenever the terrain begins to exceed your comfort zone). Likewise, the full loop can be done with a car shuttle or very simply with one vehicle if you're willing to hoof the extra 2.0 miles along the road between trailheads.

GETTING THERE: From Kanab, drive 9.0 miles east on Highway 89 to the junction of Johnson Canyon Road and go left (north). Drive 16 miles until the road turns to dirt and the signed turn for Skutumpah Road. Turn right and drive another 24 miles along this scenic back way until you arrive at the parking area next to the signed Bull Valley Gorge. The Willis Creek Trailhead is another 2.0 miles farther down Skutumpah Road.

Pleasant pastures in Sheep Creek Canyon.

Willis Creek Narrows.

THE ROUTE: Both of these hikes can be done as single out-and-back hikes from their respective trailheads. Bull Valley Gorge is much more demanding in almost every way than Willis, and offers canyoneers a fun, difficult, but non-technical day in a stunning slot. Willis on the other hand is usually done as a 4.0-mile round trip out-and-back, offering no obstacles and large impressive narrows with running water. The link up via Sheep Creek can be done either in one long day or an easy overnighter. We highly recommend starting at Bull Valley Gorge and exiting via Willis, as Bull Valley Gorge contains obstacles that may prove too difficult for many to get back up.

If doing the loop, we also recommend parking at Willis Trailhead and hiking the 2.0 road miles before your long day in the canyon. You will appreciate this when you finally claw your way back to the trailhead after a long day of underestimating canyon country, and you don't have to do the road section when you're trashed.

From the parking area at Bull Valley Gorge, head upcanyon (northwest) on the easy to follow footpath on the northeast rim for about 0.5 mile. Others may need to travel farther to find a safe place to descend to the canyon floor. Once you make it down, turn downcanyon where you will be greeted with a 10- or 12-foot dryfall, likely into a pool depending on how much water is in the canyon. This is a good test for hikers attempting Bull Valley Gorge, for if you don't feel comfortable with the awkward stemming and likely butt slide into the freezing pool below, you likely won't enjoy what lies ahead and may want to just appreciate the gorge from the rim. As always, a small rope or close friend helps immensely. Once down the falls, continue downcanyon navigating the obstacles, none of which are harder than that first dryfall, until you arrive back at the bridge and the famous stuck truck.

Continue down the gorge, scrambling, hiking, swimming, and wading through the muck until finally after a couple of

A twisted romance gazing upon walls of stone.

If walls appear to be closing in—it's because they are.

miles, the canyon opens up and the going eases up. Around 7.0 miles from whence you started, the canyon will begin to narrow again and Sheep Creek will join from the left. It's worth noting here that even if there is water in Willis Creek, don't depend on or expect it. The wash will likely be dry, as the water that flows through Willis Creek is absorbed and spread out in the much larger Sheep Creek upon arrival. Besides this confluence being in a narrow section of canyon, it is also easily identifiable as it is the first *major* canyon that comes in from the left as you descend Bull Valley Gorge.

For those looking to add a few miles to their trip, you can bypass Sheep Creek and head down to the confluence with the Paria River, then turn around and head up Sheep Creek afterward. Once in Sheep Creek, head upcanyon for a few miles until the canyon splits. Going right will keep you in Sheep Creek and eventually lead to the Sheep Creek Trailhead on Skutumpah Road. The left fork is our route, Willis Creek, which should have flowing water, and lots of human tracks. From here the hike is an easy meandering upcanyon, through the Willis Narrows and back to your car.

N
To Cannonville
Skutumpuh Rd
Willis Creek Trailhead
Willis Creek
Sheep Creek
Willis/Sheep Creek Confluence
Bull Valley Gorge Trailhead
Skutumpuh Road
Skutumpuh Rd
To Kanab
Bull Valley Gorge
Sheep Creek
BVG & Sheep Confluence
To Paria River
0
0.5
1.0
1.5
2.0 miles
6200
6400
6600

22. Lick Wash

DISTRICT:	Grand Staircase/Skutumpah Rd.
RATING:	Easy
DISTANCE:	4–8 miles
ELEVATION GAIN:	Negligible
ROUND-TRIP TIME:	2–6 hours
MAP:	Trails Illustrated #714, Grand Staircase Paunsaugunt Plateau
NEAREST LANDMARK:	Paria River

COMMENT: Tucked between the Pink and White Cliffs, the Lick Wash narrows are diagonally striped with a grayish-golden tint.

This out-and-back route leaves the distance up to you, but there are some unique rock formations (the Lost Spire Hoo-doo) downcanyon that make exploring beyond the end of the narrows enticing. The true end is a wide sandy wash that converges with Park Wash. There is no reliable water source on this hike.

Choose your own turnaround near the end of Lick Wash.

GETTING THERE: From Kanab, drive 9.0 miles east on Highway 89 to the junction of Johnson Canyon Road and go left (north). Drive 16 miles until the road turns to dirt and the signed turn for Skutumpah Road. Turn right and drive another 14 miles along this scenic back way until you arrive at the signed trailhead for Lick Wash.

From Escalante, drive 34 miles east on Highway 12 until you reach Cannonville. Turn left (south) on Kodachrome Road/Main Street and go 3.0 miles until you see the signed turnoff for Skutumpah Road. Turn right on this dirt road and follow it for another 18 miles until you arrive at the signed trailhead for Lick Wash.

THE ROUTE: About 0.25 mile downstream from the trailhead, the canyon narrows up into an interesting array of rock features and side canyons. Given this canyon is higher in elevation than many of the other slot canyons in this book, you have the opportunity to explore

The fiery tip of Lost Spire Hoodoo.

Move with the bend of the canyon walls.

Sharp sea of stacked sandstone.

Slitherin' Slot.

new flora and fauna found in the higher biomes. Meander your way down-canyon for a couple of miles until the narrows open up and the walls extend in height. You can choose to head back to your car from here or continue to explore Lick Wash all the way down to Park Wash and the sky island plateau of No Man's Mesa. The real fun of lower Lick Wash lies in exploring the upper slickrock benches and side canyons. Follow the red-capped hoodoo beacons for an adventure up to The Lost Spire and the Slytherin' Slot amidst a sea of white Navajo Sandstone.

LICK WASH
N
To Cannonville
Skutumpuh Rd
Lick Wash Trailhead
Skutumpuh Rd
To Kanab
Lick Wash Trail
Park Wash
No Man's Mesa
0
0.5
1.0
1.5
2.0 miles

23. Wahweap Hoodoos

DISTRICT:	Highway 89 Corridor, Kanab to Page
RATING:	Easy
DISTANCE:	8 miles
ELEVATION GAIN:	300 feet
ROUND-TRIP TIME:	3–6 hours
MAP:	Trails Illustrated #714, Grand Staircase Paunsaugunt Plateau
NEAREST LANDMARK:	Lake Powell

COMMENT: Leave your chitchat at the trailhead and listen to the sounds of the "Towers of Silence" as you wander among an outcropping of mysterious sandstone spires. The science fiction strange structures adjacent to Wahweap Creek are formed when the softer Entrada Sandstone, which comprises the white stalks, erodes beneath the harder rock of the orange caps (look close to see they are actually a conglomeration of a variety of rocks).

Delicate details dressed in white.

The Towers Of Silence.

There are three sections, or coves, of hoodoos: the Riverside Cove, Hoodoo Central, and the Towers of Silence. Each cove and hoodoo is unique, so plan additional time for this hike to take in, appreciate, and contemplate their details.

There are faint boot-beaten paths around the hoodoos but no set route. Please be respectful of these delicate rock formations (look but don't touch or climb) and the surrounding cryptobiotic soil (tread lightly and avoid walking through it when at all possible).

GETTING THERE: From Page, Arizona, go west on Highway 89 for about 16 miles to the small town of Big Water. Turn right on Fish Hatchery Road, which will turn to dirt shortly after passing through Big Water. Stay left, and follow the dirt road passing the fish hatchery and crossing Wahweap Creek and park at the signed trailhead for the hoodoos about 4.0 miles from the highway.

THE ROUTE: From the trailhead, follow the trail markers up the road about 100 yards and turn left into Wahweap Creek.

Some things are best left to the imagination.

From here just head upcreek, choosing whichever route suits you. This will likely be determined by how much water is in the creek, which can vary greatly depending on the season and/or recent storms. A couple miles into the hike you will come upon a large side canyon and drainage on your left. This is Lower Sidestep Canyon. For those looking to explore, this canyon offers a great opportunity and will eventually get you to Upper Sidestep, and the White Rock Hoodoos. Continuing up Wahweap Creek, the first of the Wahweap Hoodoos (the Riverside Cove) will be visible below the cliff band on your left, about 4.0 miles from the trailhead. While many people turn around here, you know better since you have this fine guidebook in your hands. Head back to the creek and continue upcanyon for a few hundred yards, around the thick brush until you find a route through to the large side canyon on the left. Continue up to explore the second set of hoodoos (Hoodoo Central). Continue even farther up Wahweap Creek to the third and final set of hoodoos (Towers of Silence) and return to your car once you have satisfied your hoodoo itch.

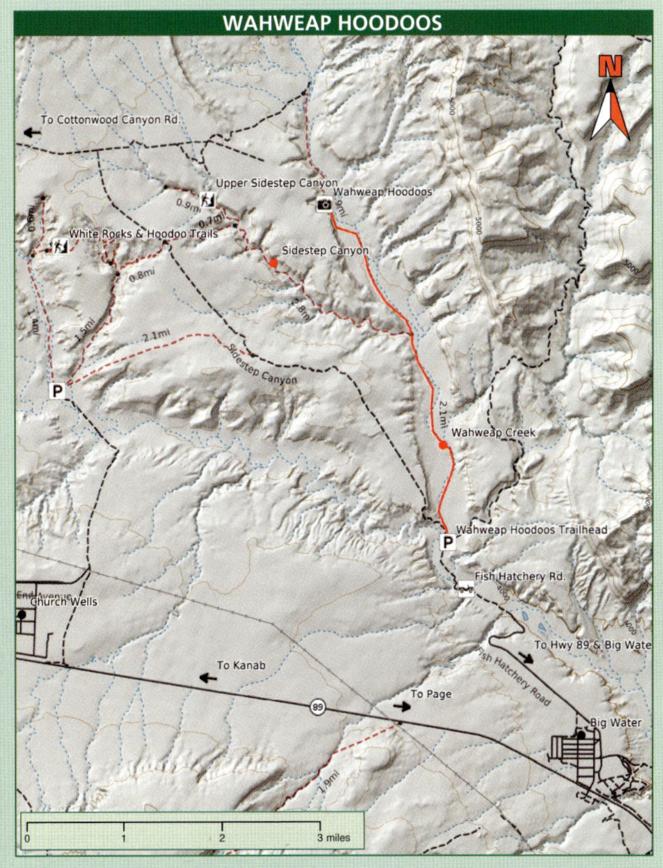

WAHWEAP HOODOOS
N
To Cottonwood Canyon Rd.
Upper Sidestep Canyon
0.9mi
Wahweap Hoodoos
0.7mi
.9mi
White Rocks & Hoodoo Trails
Sidestep Canyon
0.6mi
0.8mi
0.8mi
1.4mi
1.5mi
2.1mi
Sidestep Canyon
2.1mi
P
Wahweap Creek
Wahweap Hoodoos Trailhead
P
Fish Hatchery Rd.
End Avenue
Church Wells
To Hwy 89 & Big Wate
To Kanab
Fish Hatchery Road
To Page
89
Big Water
1.9mi
0   1   2   3 miles

24. Buckskin Gulch via Wire Pass

DISTRICT:	Highway 89 Corridor, Kanab to Page
RATING:	Difficult
DISTANCE:	24 miles
ELEVATION GAIN:	800 feet
ROUND-TRIP TIME:	1–2 days
MAP:	Trails Illustrated #859 Paria Canyon, Kanab
NEAREST LANDMARK:	The Paria River

COMMENT: At approximately 16 miles, Buckskin Gulch is considered the longest slot canyon in the Southwest. Distance aside, the canyon is equally spectacular for its tight corridors (less than 10 feet wide at its narrows, which extend for 13 miles) and depth (up to 500 feet). This route begins at Wire Pass, another stunning slot canyon in its own right, before joining with Buckskin Gulch proper all the way to the Paria River confluence, ending at the White House Trail.

Standing geometry in Slide Rock Arch.

Do not let the beauty of this route distract you from its perils, as this is considered one of the most dangerous hikes in the U.S. The threat of flash floods is high, especially during late summer monsoons, the opportunities for exit in case of emergency are limited, and the obstacles are numerous. Expect to encounter slick mud, deep pools of water, river walking and several spots that require down-climbing (including a drop-off with a fixed rope). At times swimming may be necessary, but typical depths range from ankle to waist deep. The pools of water remain cold year-round and sun exposure is limited—bring extra layers for this hike! When not wading in water, expect to traipse over melon-sized boulders and through long stretches of both wet and dry sand.

A car shuttle is required for this hike—leave one at the White House Trailhead (this is where you will finish) and park your other vehicle at the Wire Pass Trailhead.

Beauty and danger at every turn.

A chance to truly see something.

To Wire Pass Trailhead: From Kanab, Utah, drive east on Highway 89 for 38 miles. Just before passing through The Cockscomb, turn right off the highway and onto House Rock Valley Road. After 4.5 miles you will see the signs for the Buckskin Gulch trailhead. This is an alternative, worthy, and slightly longer option to the route described in this book. Continue on House Rock Valley Road for 4.0 more miles and park at the signed Wire Pass trailhead.

From Page, Arizona, drive west on Highway 89 for 34 miles. Just after passing through The Cockscomb, turn left off the highway and onto House Rock Valley Road. Follow the directions above until you arrive at the Wire Pass trailhead.

To White House Trailhead: From Kanab, Utah, drive east on Highway 89 for 43 miles. Turn right onto White House Trailhead Road, keeping an eye out for BLM Paria Contact Station signs. Head south for about 2.0 miles and either pick a designated campsite or park outside the campground for dayhikes and shuttles.

From Page, Arizona, drive west on Highway 89 for 29 miles, and turn left onto White House Trailhead Road. Follow directions about until you arrive at the trailhead.

THE ROUTE: Starting at Wire Pass, cross the dirt road from the parking lot to where the trailhead begins. The path is well marked and jumps in and out of single track and sandy washes for about a mile. Here Wire Canyon narrows (at some points it is only 3 feet wide) and you will encounter a small log/boulder jam early on in this 0.5-mile long slot canyon. The canyon wid-

Consumed by color.

ens just before the confluence with Buckskin Gulch—the south side of the canyon walls contain petroglyphs depicting bighorn sheep.

Head downcanyon, following the twists and turns in the canyon for the next 16 miles. Expect varying amounts of mud, water, and debris in these sections. The route remains non-technical until you get 1.5 miles from the end of the gulch, where you will encounter a large pile of over-sized boulders, roughly 20 feet high, and two options to get around them. The first is to stay high on the left side of the canyon and descend a set of Moki steps. It is also possible to get down by crawling below a set of boulders in the center of the canyon.

The Paria River confluence marks the first major change in direction since the first 2.0 miles of this route. Head upriver, likely hiking straight into the pale jade green waters encapsulated by this colorful corridor (or a long stretch dry and muddy riverbed if it is not flowing). Water levels will vary dramatically but prepare for around 7.0 miles of river walking and crossing until a single track use-trail cuts away from the riverbed leading to the White House Trailhead and your vehicle.

To Page
To Page
White House Trailhead & Campground
Paria Canyon
1.9mi
1.0mi
2.9mi
Johnson Store
Buckskin Gulch
UtahKane
Wolf Knoll
Steamboat
Arizona
Coconino
Hwy 89
To Kanab and Hwy 89
To Kanab
Buckskin Gulch Trailhead
House Rock Valley Rd.
House Rock Valley Road
Cocks Comb
Fivemile
6.8mi
Wire Pass Trailhead
House Rock Valley Road
1.7mi
1.3mi
3.8mi
UtahKane
Coconino
Jug
Top
5 miles
4
3
2
1
0

25. Kitchen Falls and Starlight Canyon

DISTRICT:	Highway 89 Corridor, Kanab to Page
RATING:	Easy
DISTANCE:	14 miles
ELEVATION GAIN:	1,000 feet
ROUND-TRIP TIME:	4–8 hours
MAP:	Trails Illustrated #714, Grand Staircase Paunsaugunt Plateau
NEAREST LANDMARK:	Paria Movie Set and The Paria River

COMMENT: Do you like long walks along sandy riverbanks between deep red canyon walls? Wading directly in the gently flowing river? Or maybe you like the spice of the occasional bushwhack or crawl through thick and thorny brush? Not ready to commit? Not to worry, with no established trails these are just a few methods you can use to work your way through the Paria River Canyon to Kitchen Canyon, Kitchen Falls, and Starlight Canyon.

Shine on down to Starlight Canyon.

From the wide expanse of Paria Canyon, Kitchen Canyon will draw in your focus as you follow the creek to Kitchen Falls, which flows periodically throughout the year, especially during spring snowmelt and after late summer rainstorms and monsoons. We witnessed the falls the day after a fall hurricane struck the Southwest (an unusual occurrence to say the least). Beware of the deep quicksand that accompanies these same conditions.

Continue onward to Starlight Canyon, which is notable for a short section of picturesque narrows with a steadily flowing spring near the end point.

This hike starts and ends at the Old Pareah Townsite (the original spelling for Paria, a Piute word meaning "muddy water"), which is across and slightly downriver from the parking area. Not much is left here, but the few old foundations might be of interest to you Mormon history buffs. This area is also home to the Paria Movie Set, which was used for a number of spaghetti westerns, but unfortunately was burned to the ground in 2006.

Be prepared to hike through water during the majority of the year. Hiking sandals or shoes that drain well are recommended.

GETTING THERE: From Kanab, Utah, head east on Highway 89 for 33 miles. Turn left (north) at the signs for the Paria Movie Set and old townsite. From here the dirt road takes you toward the Paria River, and after a few miles you will arrive at the Paria Movie Set. The road then crosses the wash and continues for another 1.0 mile through deep sand to park at the roundabout right at the river. Take care to stay on the actual road as many people mistakenly drive directly through the wash.

From Page, Arizona, head west on Highway 89 for 39 miles. Turn right (north) at the signs for the Paria Movie Set and old townsite and follow the directions above.

THE ROUTE: Once at the parking area, start upcanyon, choosing the route that seems best. The Paria is known for dramatic fluctuations in water level, so be prepared for hot and dry conditions, or a muddy monsoon-fueled torrent that sends desert river rats into a packrafting frenzy. Kitchen Canyon is the third canyon coming in from the left, upriver of the townsite. About 4.0 miles from your car you will head up Kitchen Canyon, which will likely have at least a trickle of water.

Kitchen Canyon Faucet.

Somewhere over the rainbow hills and yellow mud ribbon.

Early autumn leaves shimmer in Starlight.

If you are wise and choose this hike after a storm, there should be a decent amount of water flowing to the confluence with the Paria. Another 1.5 miles up the scenic Kitchen Canyon and you will dead-end at the waterfall.

From the waterfall, turn back downcanyon and immediately turn right up Starlight Canyon. The narrows come into view eventually, and you can either continue exploring the upper reaches of Starlight or begin the trek back.

For those looking for an even longer day, or wishing to turn your hike into an overnighter, it is easy to continue up the Paria for about 1.0 mile or so, then turn right into the seldom visited Hogeye Canyon. An out-and-back exploration of Hogeye, or an even further link-up of the Paria to Hogeye to Lower Hackberry is possible—dare we say, recommended.

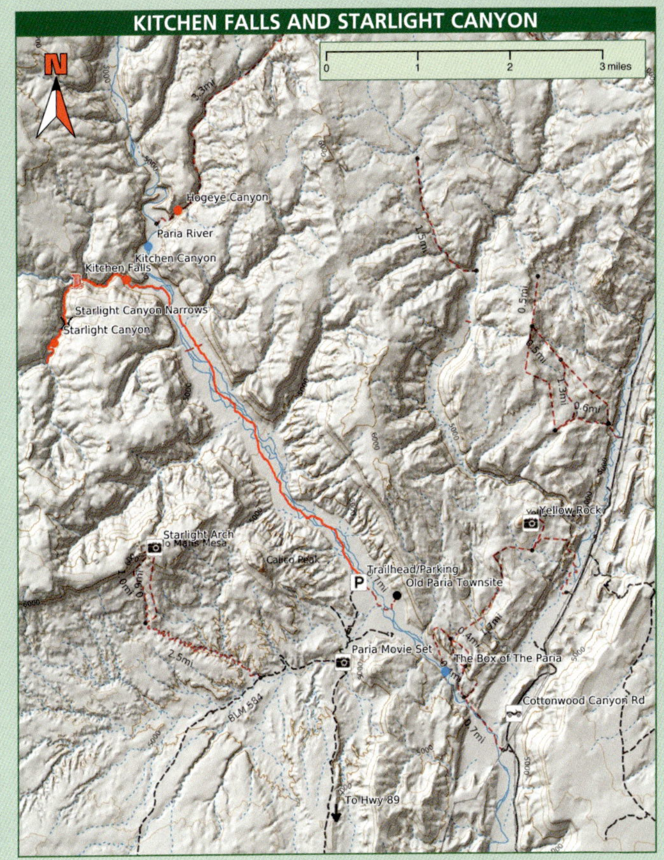
N
0
1
2
3 miles
3.3mi
Hogeye Canyon
Paria River
Kitchen Canyon
Kitchen Falls
Starlight Canyon Narrows
Starlight Canyon
1.5mi
0.5mi
0.5mi
1.3mi
0.6mi
Yellow Rock
Starlight Arch
To Mans Mesa
Calico Peak
Trailhead/Parking
Old Paria Townsite
1mi
P
1.0mi
0.6mi
2.5mi
0.4mi
1mi
The Box of The Paria
Paria Movie Set
BLM 585
Cottonwood Canyon Rd
0.7mi
To Hwy 89

About the Authors

Morgan Sjogren is a freelance writer and photographer whose storytelling focuses on human-powered exploration and wild landscapes. Sjogren's book debut, *The Best Bears Ears National Monument Hikes* (2018), was the first guidebook devoted to the national monument after its 2016 designation. Morgan wrote *Outlandish: Fuel Your Epic*, a collection of misadventure essays and culinary concoctions, concurrently with this guidebook. A passionate advocate for public lands, Morgan is a nomad roaming the Southwest.

Michael VerSteeg is a Southwestern native who has spent most of his life exploring the Four Corners region. He lives in his cabin on the backside of Granite Mountain in central Arizona.

Checklist

Illustration by Jesse Crock

Join Today.
Adventure Tomorrow.

The Colorado Mountain Club is the Rocky Mountain community for mountain education, adventure, and conservation. We bring people together to share our love of the mountains. We value our community and go out of our way to welcome and include all Coloradoans—from the uninitiated to the expert, there is a place for everyone here.

www.cmc.org